TWO MEMOIRS

OF

RENAISSANCE FLORENCE

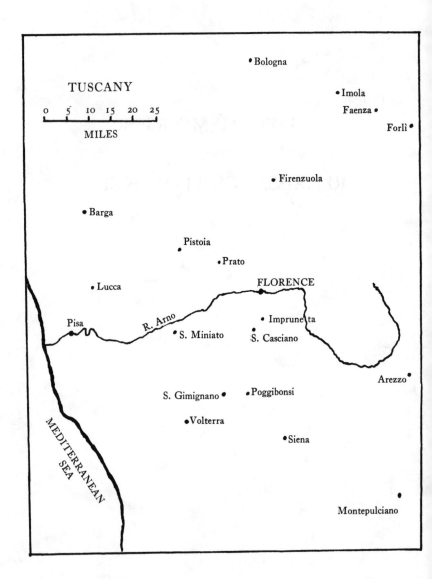

TUSCANY

0   5   10   15   20   25

MILES

• Bologna

• Imola

Faenza •

Forlì •

• Firenzuola

• Barga

Pistoia
•

• Prato

• Lucca

FLORENCE

Pisa
•

R. Arno

• S. Miniato

• Imprunetta

S. Casciano

Arezzo •

S. Gimignano •

• Poggibonsi

• Volterra

• Siena

MEDITERRANEAN
SEA

•
Montepulciano

TWO MEMOIRS

OF

RENAISSANCE FLORENCE

The Diaries of

Buonaccorso Pitti and Gregorio Dati

TRANSLATED BY JULIA MARTINES

Edited by GENE BRUCKER

Prospect Heights, Illinois

WINGATE UNIVERSITY LIBRARY

For information about this book, write or call:
Waveland Press, Inc.
P.O. Box 400
Prospect Heights, Illinois 60070
(847) 634-0081

Copyright © 1967 by Gene A. Brucker
1991 reissued by Waveland Press, Inc.

ISBN 0-88133-622-X

All rights reserved. No part of this book may be reproduced, stored in a retrieval system, or transmitted in any form or by any means without permission in writing from the publisher.

Printed in the United States of America

7 6 5

Contents

Preface

THE translation of these memoirs by Julia Martines has been made from printed texts. The most recent edition of the Pitti memoir is *Cronica di Buonaccorso Pitti con annotazioni ristampata da Alberto Bacchi della Lega* [*Collezione di opere inedite o rare*, 93], published by Romagnoli-Dall'Acqua (Bologna, 1905). An earlier, incomplete edition of Pitti's work was published by Manni (Florence, 1720). Gregorio Dati's diary was edited by Carlo Gargiolli, *Il libro segreto di Gregorio Dati* [*Scelta di curiosità letterarie inedite o rare dal secolo XIII al XVII*, 102], published by Gaetano Romagnoli (Bologna, 1865).

Both of these memoirs have been abridged in this translation. The excised material includes some genealogical data on members of the Pitti family, descriptions of minor offices held by Pitti and Dati, and some fragments from the business accounts of Dati's companies. The translated portions of the Pitti memoir are printed on the following pages of the Bacchi della Lega edition: 7–10, 16–17, 33–163, 165–184, 189–195, 206, 230–235, 240–242. These pages of Dati's *libro segreto* (in the Gargiolli edition) have been translated: 11–14, 16–20, 26–48, 51–62, 68–84, 87–90, 96–107, 110, 113–120.

Until the middle of the eighteenth century, Florentines changed the number of the year not on the first day of January, but three months later, on the feast of the Annunciation (25 March). In this translation, the dates have all been converted to the modern style. Some attempt has also been made to systematize the spelling of both Christian

names and surnames. Pitti and Dati learned to write Italian
without benefit of dictionaries, grammars or courses in
orthography.

A useful survey of Florentine history is Ferdinand
Schevill, *Medieval and Renaissance Florence,* Harper
Torchbook edition, two volumes (New York, 1963). The
best introduction to Florentine society in the late fourteenth and early fifteenth centuries is the book by Lauro
Martines, *The Social World of the Florentine Humanists
1390–1460* (Princeton, 1963). Information on the business
world and the society of the Arno city may be gleaned from
Raymond de Roover, *The Rise and Decline of the Medici
Bank 1397–1494* (Cambridge, Mass., 1963), and Iris
Origo, *The Merchant of Prato* (New York, 1957). Among
the books which may be consulted for political and institu-
tional history are: Hans Baron, *The Crisis of the Early
Italian Renaissance,* 2nd edition (Princeton, 1966); Gene
Brucker, *Florentine Politics and Society, 1343–1378*
(Princeton, 1962); Charles Bayley, *War and Society in
Renaissance Florence: the De Militia of Leonardo Bruni*
(Toronto, 1961); and Nicolai Rubinstein, *The Govern-
ment of Florence under the Medici 1434–1494* (Oxford,
1966).

GENE BRUCKER

Berkeley, California
August, 1966

Introduction:

Florentine Diaries and Diarists

by Gene Brucker

THE memoirs of Buonaccorso Pitti and Gregorio Dati are notable examples of a common literary form in Renaissance Florence. More than one hundred private diaries or *ricordanze* written between the fourteenth and the sixteenth centuries survive in the State Archives and libraries, and in the possession of noble families. The literary and historical interest of these memoirs vary widely, but some—like the writings translated here—throw light upon both the public and the private dimensions of the Florentine experience. These Tuscan memoirs constitute one of the largest collections of private diaries in Europe before the French began to develop this form in the sixteenth century. They deserve study, therefore, as an early and important chapter in the history of that peculiarly European genre, the autobiography.

The origins of these diaries can be traced directly to the secret account books of Florentine businessmen. Merchants and property owners customarily kept records of their economic activities: books of receipts and expenses, records of commercial transactions, copies of property sales, testaments. Normally, one ledger would be designated as a *libro segreto,* a "secret book," and in this volume the merchant would record information of particular significance for himself and his heirs which he did not wish to reveal to outsid-

ers. Typical examples of these *libri segreti* from the fourteenth century are found in the records of mercantile companies edited by Professor Sapori.[1] Most of the information recorded in these ledgers pertained to economic affairs:
business partnerships, capital investments, dowries. Occasionally, however, these volumes contain information of a
different nature: references to political events, to a pestilence or flood, or to some significant private experience. In
the Peruzzi account books, for example, are entries by
Simone di Rinieri Peruzzi, one of which described his experiences as a Florentine diplomat at the outbreak of the
war with the Papacy in 1375, and another in which he
denounced his son Benedetto: "May he be accursed by God,
amen! And if he survives me, and I have not punished him
as he deserves, may the just sentence of God chastise him
according to his deserts as a vile traitor!"[2] From such
random comments, we can add to our stock of information
about political events, and also gain some revealing insights
into the value systems of literate Florentines.

Examples of these memoirs, very rare before 1350, become increasingly numerous in the late decades of the fourteenth century. Among the Medici papers in the State Archives in Florence is a diary compiled by Foligno di Conte
de' Medici in the 1360's and 1370's, which contains valuable data on the condition of that family before it achieved
its dominant position in the fifteenth century. An interesting
diary of the 1380's was written by Paolo Sassetti which
contains lively accounts of his relations with relatives and
neighbors as well as his reaction to important public events.
The fullest autobiographical statement which has survived
from the fourteenth century is the "domestic chronicle" of
the lawyer, Donato Velluti (d. 1370).[3] His diary is a

[1] *I libri di commercio dei Peruzzi* (Milan, 1934); *I libri della ragione ban-
caria dei Gianfigliazzi* (Milan 1943); *I libri degli Alberti del Giudice*
(Milan, 1952).

[2] *I libri di commercio dei Peruzzi,* p. 522.

[3] *La cronica domestica di Messer Donato Velluti,* eds. I. del Lungo and
G. Volpi (Florence, 1914). The Medici diary is in the *Archivio di Stato di
Firenze* [*ASF*], *Archivio Mediceo avanti il Principato,* 152. The Sassetti

mine of information about Florentine public life after the
Black Death, for he played an important role in communal
politics. Equally valuable for the historian are Velluti's
references to his family and to his own career as a lawyer
and politician. His *ricordanze* include brief biographies of
his relatives, in which he makes some interesting—if rather
primitive—attempts at character portrayal. While com-
menting upon the events and personalities of his age, Velluti
unconsciously reveals much about himself: his values, the
mores of his class, the ideals and aspirations which motivated him and his fellow-citizens.

Velluti's diary is very different in form and character
from the typical *libro segreto*. It is more detailed, more
elaborate, and above all, more personal. It reflects significant changes in the social and intellectual climate in four-
teenth-century Florence, and particularly, changes in the
patriciate's conception of itself. The rationale for compil-
ing memoirs was often formulated in terms of family interest: to pass on to later generations the experiences of the
writer and his contemporaries, to demonstrate by illustra-
tion and example which paths to follow and which to avoid.
Another motive was family pride. These diarists wished
to set down the facts of their family's antiquity; they also
described the exploits of its distinguished members, the
prominent offices held, the honorable marriages contracted.
And though not so blatantly displayed as in Cellini's autobiography a century later, the element of self-aggrandize-
ment was certainly present in these personalized *ricordanze*
of the late fourteenth and fifteenth centuries.

The most puzzling aspect of these memoirs is the Florentine monopoly. Why do scores of diaries exist in Florentine repositories, while only a handful have been discovered
in other Italian cities? The simplest explanation is the acci-
dent of survival. After working for a decade in Ligurian

diary is in *ASF, Carte Strozziane,* series II, 4. Several unedited diaries of
the fourteenth century are described by P. J. Jones, "Florentine Families
and Florentine Diaries in the Fourteenth Century," in *Papers of the British
School at Rome,* XXIV (1956), 183–205.

archives on his study of fifteenth century Genoa, Jacques Heers could find only one merchant's account book.[4] Given the highly developed commercial economy in that port city, one can only conclude that these records, together with other private documents, were simply destroyed, and that the highly unstable political and social conditions in Genoa probably account for most of these losses. But this explanation will not hold for Venice, with its centuries of relatively placid internal history, and its corps of noble families deeply concerned about their—and their city's—past. Did Venetian patricians write memoirs, and if so, why have they not survived? Did they refrain from writing personal diaries because of their fear of the inquisitiorial magistracy, the Council of Ten? Or was this caution rather the consequence of a system of training and education which stressed group action and achievement, and regarded individual striving for fame and glory with suspicion? Whatever the explanation for the paucity of diaries elsewhere, it seems clear that social and political conditions in Florence were particularly conducive to the writing of memoirs. This milieu was relatively free, yet charged with tension; and this combination apparently stimulated those qualities of imagination, insight and curiosity which found expression in these diaries.

The authors of the two private chronicles here were contemporaries; their lifetimes spanned nearly identical periods. As adults, they were witnesses to one of the most creative half-centuries (1380–1430) in Florentine history. But their testimony concerning this age is fragmentary, for they were writing private documents and were not attempting, as were the Villani brothers in their chronicles, to record for posterity the total achievement of their native city.

Pitti and Dati were businessmen, and it is about this aspect of Florentine life that they are most informative. Buonaccorso Pitti began his career as an international trader and for some years operated as a professional gambler in the princely courts of France and the Low

[4] J. Heers, *Gênes au XV͏ᵉ siècle* (Paris, 1961), p. 5.

Countries. After a decade in this exotic profession, he returned to Florence to pursue the more sedate occupation of cloth manufacturer. Gregorio Dati's business interests were more conservative; his main activity was the manufacture and sale of silk cloth. This industry expanded in Florence during the fifteenth century, and the rise in Dati's economic fortunes is partly explained by his involvement in an industry which, in modern parlance, possessed "growth potential."

Two characteristic features of Florentine business activity, its variety and its vicissitudes, are well illustrated by these diaries. While living abroad, Pitti not only gambled but loaned money to impecunious gamblers; he bought and sold jewels, horses, cargoes of saffron and wine. Dati's business activities were less varied, but they too included a stint in a woolen cloth shop, the management of a silk shop, and partnerships in trading companies operating in Aragon and Catalonia. Dati's career was in the classic "rags to riches" tradition, but the path to wealth was not smooth. Profits gained in silk cloth manufacture were dissipated in the Spanish trade, where losses occurred as the result of shipwreck, piracy, bad debts to princes, and poor management. Toward the end of his life, Dati was saved from bankruptcy by a timely loan from his brother Lionardo, the General of the Dominican Order. Faintly visible in these fluctuations of individual fortunes are the swings of the economic pendulum involving the entire business community in Florence. In the decade after 1375, when Pitti and Dati were embarking upon their business careers, Florence was buffeted by a combination of misfortunes— wars, internal upheavals, pestilence, famine—which seriously damaged the economy. War was the greatest enemy of the business community; it disrupted trade routes, closed off markets and devoured profits. In 1414, the end of a series of exhausting struggles with the city's formidable antagonists, Giangaleazzo Visconti of Milan (d. 1402) and King Ladislaus of Naples (d. 1414), ushered in a period of prosperity which continued for a decade. But this was followed by another long and enervating conflict with the lord of Milan, Filippo Maria Visconti, which imposed severe strains upon the economy and the political order.

There are some references in these diaries to the political events which the authors witnessed. They illustrate significant aspects of Florentine political experience, both internally and in the wider arena of foreign affairs. Pitti's accounts of his diplomatic missions to France and Germany are episodes in the city's wars with Giangaleazzo Visconti. In 1402, the Milanese ruler had gained control of territory surrounding Florence and was preparing a final assault on the beleaguered city when he fell sick and died. Pitti was also involved in the bitter partisan dispute over the city's relations with another enemy, Ladislaus of Naples. As a member of that faction which favored peace with the Angevin monarch, Pitti aroused the hostility of the war party, whose members were convinced that Florence could never live peacefully with Ladislaus. Dati's memoirs throw little light upon these events, but he was an interested spectator. He wrote a history of Florence's struggles with Giangaleazzo, a patriotic account which eulogized the city's steadfast resistance to the Milanese despot. He also charted the expansion of Florentine territory.[5] For it was during the lifetime of these men that the city's dominion nearly doubled in size, incorporating the Tuscan towns of Arezzo, Montepulciano. Pisa, Cortona and Livorno.

Pitti's diary contains some interesting details of the political conflicts in Florence during his youth. He was an active participant in the 1378 disorders, during the Ciompi revolution, when the city was governed for six weeks by a group of artisans and cloth workers. Having fallen out of sympathy with the regime which controlled the city from 1378 to 1382, he went into exile and joined in conspiracies to overthrow that popular government. The regime established in 1382 was dominated by a coterie of wealthy and

---

[5] *L'istoria di Firenze dal 1380 al 1405,* ed. L. Pratesi (Norcia, 1904). For an analysis of this history, see H. Baron, *The Crisis of the Early Italian Renaissance,* 2nd edition (Princeton, 1966), ch. 8.

influential families: the Albizzi, Strozzi, Peruzzi, Capponi. It resisted numerous attempts by malcontents to overthrow it, becoming more oligarchic in character after each unsuccessful coup. The lesser elements of the guild community, the artisans and small shopkeepers, retained a nominal share of offices, but political power was concentrated in the hands of the great mercantile families. But Florence never became a monolithic dictatorship. Although the governing class was limited in size, it did include representatives from more than 100 families who held offices and participated in the formulation of policy. Moreover, the system remained flexible enough to permit small infusions of new blood, as the career of Gregorio Dati illustrated. For he was a "new man" from a small family of modest status who—in 1429—was chosen Standard-bearer of Justice, the republic's highest office.

From these memoirs one might conclude that these two men, as representatives of Florence's governing class, were totally oblivious to the cultural revolution which took place during their lifetimes. They were, after all, contemporaries of the distinguished humanists, Coluccio Salutati and Lionardo Bruni. They witnessed the construction of Brunelleschi's dome for the Cathedral and Ghiberti's Baptistery doors. They may well have observed Masaccio at work in the Brancacci chapel; the Carmine church was not far from their parish of S. Felice in Piazza. Their failure to mention these men and their achievements, of which they were certainly aware, was due primarily to the private nature of their diaries. Only if Brunelleschi or Masaccio had been employed to build or decorate their family chapel would they have described their artistic accomplishments. But another reason for their silence was the status of literary and artistic production in the value system of the Florentine patriciate. Creations of artists and writers were prized, certainly, or they would never have been subsidized by this society. But for Pitti and Dati, and for most of their contemporaries, the works of Bruni and Donatello were not as important as their private business affairs, or the republic's conquest of Pisa. Renaissance Florence was inhabited by individuals who, like most men at most times, placed the greatest importance upon visible, tangible, material objectives, and who thought first of themselves and their own interests.

The tax records (*catasto*) of 1427 provide valuable information on the economic condition of these two diarists. The statements of resources and liabilities which Pitti and Dati submitted to the tax authorities reveal some striking similarities in their economic status. Neither were among the wealthiest residents of their district of Ferza, in the quarter of S. Spirito.[6] Both men possessed assets (not including their tax-exempt residence) in excess of 3,000 florins. This would be equivalent to $12,000 at the current gold price of $35 per ounce; in terms of contemporary purchasing power, it was worth more than $60,000. The property holdings of both were diversified. Pitti owned three houses in his parish, a cloth-stretching shed, and two farms in the contado (the valley of the Pesa river). Included in Dati's portfolio of possessions were eight houses and cottages within the city walls: four in his own parish of S. Felice, the rest scattered in working-class districts on the south side of the Arno. Dati also owned three farms in the contado which yielded sufficient grain, oil and wine for his family. In addition to these real estate investments, both merchants had lent several hundred florins to merchants, and also owned shares of the Monte, the commune's funded debt, which yielded a low but regular return of interest. In 1427, Pitti was no longer engaged in cloth manufacturing, while Dati had invested 468 florins in a silk company which he operated with two partners.

[6] These tax declarations are in *ASF, Catasto,* 66, fols. 154v–156r (Pitti), 469v–472r (Dati). Pitti calculated his taxable assets at 3,011 florins; his debts amounted to 1,188 fl., and his fifteen dependents gave him an additional 3,000 fl. in deductions. His liabilities were thus greater than his assets, and the *catasto* officials assessed him 1 fl., 10 *soldi*. Dati's total assets were 3,368 fl., his obligations (including dependents), 3,689 fl. His assessment was fixed at 3 fl.

The Pitti and Dati households were large; their size permitted both men to claim substantial tax deductions of 200 florins for each dependent. Buonaccorso Pitti's household of fifteen members included two married sons and their families, as well as five of his adolescent children. Gregorio Dati listed twelve dependents: his wife, sister and nine children. The provision of dowries for his five daughters, aged one to thirteen, must have been Gregorio Dati's most serious concern in his last years, for a minimum of 500 florins was required to contract an honorable marriage with a good family.

These statistics indicate surface similarities in age, wealth, investments and family structure. They do not reveal the significant contrasts between these men, who had both gained modest fortunes and enjoyed political careers of some distinction. The fundamental difference was social background. Pitti belonged to one of the city's aristocratic families. For more than a century his ancestors had played an important role in the Florentine business world, had filled the commune's highest offices, and had intermarried with other prominent families. While the Pitti could not match the antiquity and prestige of their enemies, the Ricasoli, they were the social equals of the Albizzi, Strozzi, Guicciardini, and Medici, all families of the first rank in the urban patriciate. By contrast, Dati's origins were very modest. In his rather pathetic attempt to trace a genealogy for himself, he goes back only two generations, to his grandfather the pursemaker, whose shop on the Ponte Vecchio was destroyed in the great flood of 1333. By dint of his own efforts, Dati's father had risen above that modest artisan status, but Gregorio himself began his mercantile career on borrowed money. His early marriages to women of unknown families were a clear sign of his low social standing. That he ultimately achieved wealth and political position was a remarkable testimony to the relatively open character of Florentine society, which did not bar ambitious and talented men from either economic or political rewards.

This difference in social origins is one factor in the contrasting temperaments displayed in the diaries. For these writings do provide clues for discerning the personalities of the authors: in their choice of themes, in their reaction to events, in their revelation—often unconscious—of their values. Of the two, Dati appears the more traditional and conservative, more representative of older values and behavior patterns. His preoccupation with economic problems is characteristic of the artisan-shopkeeper mentality; his pious articulation of religious maxims also marks him as belonging to an older generation. In politics, he was never a leader but a follower. He embodied the traditional political virtues of loyalty, patriotism and service, which were always idealized, though not invariably followed, by the Florentine patriciate.

Buonaccorso Pitti was a very different type. Although travel and residence in foreign lands were common experiences of the Florentine entrepreneurial class, Pitti's career abroad was unique. Few Italians in the late fourteenth century were so well known at the French royal court, or were on such familiar terms with the higher ranks of Europe's aristocracy. Pitti became so intimately acquainted with this princely milieu that he seems to have absorbed the mores and values of the French aristocracy. But the arrogance or *grandigia* which he frequently displayed in his social relationships was characteristic of the Florentine patriciate in this period. Pride and enterprise were Pitti's most distinctive traits. They invite comparison with the qualities displayed by that Florentine hero of a later generation, Benvenuto Cellini. There are certain similarities in their behavior patterns, in the ways in which they view themselves and their world. The differences between the two diarists, which are striking and important, indicate some of the changes which had occurred in Florence between 1400 and 1530.

The Diary of Buonaccorso Pitti

THE year of Our Lord 1412. In this year I, Buonaccorso Pitti, being a descendant of Buonsignore Pitti—
through his son, also Buonsignore, whose son, Maffeo, had
a son, Buonaccorso, whose son was my own father, Neri—
began to keep this diary. It has been my aim to record here
everything I could discover about our lineage and family
connections down to those formed in my own day. If I have
been unable to trace our history back to its very beginnings,
it is the fault of a kinsman of mine who had our family
papers in his keeping. This was Cioro, a descendant,
through his father, Lapo son of Maffeo, of the first Buonsignore. Cioro was such a scandalmonger that he could
never be trusted with a public appointment. He was also
notoriously envious, and when he saw us, Neri's sons, serving in some of the most illustrious offices of the Commune,
he grew bitterly envious and blamed us, quite unjustly, for
his own lack of preferment. Convinced that we had
wronged him, he made a will leaving everything to a
daughter who is now in a convent at Portico. After his
death, and while she was still living at home, we went to
see her and asked to see the family papers and registers
her father must have left. She replied that she knew nothing about them, adding that Cioro had been in the habit of
selling quantities of documents and that, shortly before
his death, she had seen him burn a great pile of papers.
She was clearly telling the truth for, although we searched
the house, we could find no trace of any papers either new

or old. This destruction of documents bearing on his own and his ancestors' lives gave the full and final measure of Cioro's rancor.

Faced with this loss, I was obliged to have recourse to papers belonging to my grandfather Buonaccorso, which were badly written and torn and generally in poor condition. However, I did find one or two things in them which I shall relate further on. I shall also record information about our forbears which I heard from my father Neri.

The main fact I have been able to establish is that the Pitti were Guelfs exiled from Semifonte by the Ghibellines who held power there.[1] After this, the family seems to have split into three branches. The first settled in Luia where their descendants today are members of prominent families and proprietors of rich estates. Their family name is Luiesi, and they are apparently the most powerful people in that area. Their connection with ourselves is proven by the fact that the emblem on their coat of arms is identical to ours. Moreover, I have heard from elders of both families that the links of kin and friendship have always been kept up.

The second branch came straight to Florence. They were known as the Ammirati and a few of them still survive in the country where they retired to live on a hill close to the site of Semifonte, which was destroyed by the Commune of Florence in 1202. This family at one time enjoyed considerable prestige in Florence and has the same armorial bearings as ourselves: a shield with black and white waves.

Finally, our own branch, the Pitti, settled in Castelvecchio in Val di Pesa,[2] where they bought some fine fertile estates and in particular a place known as *Alle Torri* on account of the two gentlemen's houses, each embellished

[1] Semifonte was a hill town near Certaldo, some thirty-five miles southwest of Florence. After its conquest in 1202, it was so completely destroyed that its exact location is unknown.

[2] The Pesa is a tributary of the Arno River, originating in the Chianti hill region south of Florence, and joining the Arno at Montelupo west of the city. The ancestral estates of the Pitti were some fifteen miles from Florence, southwest of S. Casciano.

with a tower and dovecote, which go with it. These lands
are in the family still although only one tower is left. The
other had to be knocked down in my own time in the interests of safety since it seemed in danger of collapsing.
Some years later our family moved to Florence where they
lived for a time in houses now belonging to the Machiavelli,
who bought them from Ciore and from Buonaccorso, son
of Maffeo Pitti.

. . .

Our father, Neri, Buonaccorso's son, made a lot of
money in the wool trade and, over a period of eleven years,
turned out hundreds of bolts of cloth which he sent mostly
to Puglia. He worked hard in the business, imported raw
wool from France, and had it made up into finished cloth
in our workshops. The last building he put up was a cloth-
stretching shed which cost about 3,500 florins. He does not
seem to have cared much for holding office under the Commune for he declined every appointment it is proper to decline, and I even recall that he formally refused the office
of Standard-bearer of the Militia. He sat twice in the Priorate.[3] He was a fine-looking man, six feet tall, not stout
but well built and muscular. He had red hair, good health,
a hot temper, and lived to be sixty-eight. May God pardon
him his sins. Monna Curradina [Buonaccorso's mother]
was a fine, handsome, dark-haired woman of medium
height who lived to be sixty-six.

I, myself—Buonaccorso—married Francesca, daughter
of Luca, son of Piero, son of Filippo degli Albizzi and, on
her mother's side, of Monna Dianora, daughter of Piero,
son of Neri del Palagio. My sister Madalena married

[3] The Priorate, or Signoria, was composed of nine citizens; it was the
chief executive magistracy of the Commune. Priors were selected by lot
for two-month terms of office. The office of Standard-bearer of the Militia
Company (*gonfaloniere della compagnia*) was a lesser executive body. The
sixteen Standard-bearers formed one of the two Colleges which advised the
Signoria, voted on all legislation, and with the Priors and members of the
other College of the Twelve Good Men (*dodici buonomini*), elected certain
officials of the Commune.

Francesco the son of Jacopo Pecori and bore him two children: Jacopo and Luca. My wife Francesca has two brothers: Piero and Niccolò. Niccolò married Lottiera, a daughter of Cardinale Rucellai and of Monna Lapa, whose father was Stefano Castellani. He has one son by this marriage: Luca Antonio.

Francesca and myself have so far had eleven children, seven of whom are living: Luca, Roberto, Curradina, Madalena, Francesco, Primavera and Neri. Primavera was called after Monna Dianora's mother who was a sister of Carlo and Smeraldo degli Strozzi.

.   .   .

Now I will give an account of the journeys I made to different parts of the world after the death of my father, Neri—may the Lord have mercy on him—on 25 April 1374.

When he died, my brothers and myself—eight of us with our mother—left Florence where a plague had broken out and took refuge at *Il Corno,* a country house of ours in Val di Pesa. While we were there, my brother Giovanni, who was twenty-seven years old, died of the plague, and so, a few days later, did our cousin Niccolò, Cione's son.

When the epidemic was over, we returned to Florence where we found that Niccolò's mother, Monna Margherita, had stripped the house they lived in and moved all their goods and valuables to the house of her sister, the mother of Niccolò and Guido del Grasso Mannelli. This did not seem right to us since her other son, Niccolò's brother Cione, was still alive and living at Venice. My brothers resolved that I should go and fetch this boy who was eighteen years old, so that he might look after his own interests. I set off accordingly for Venice and, on the return journey with Cione, rode out from Pietramala on St. Andrew's day. By the time we had crossed the marshes, we were so cold that we had to get off our horses. Cione, who was standing behind his, lashed at it with his whip, whereupon the nag gave him such a kick on the head that he fell into a swoon.

As there was a church nearby I was able to have Cione put into a litter and carried to Firenzuola. I wrote to Florence at once to tell my brothers what had occurred. They told his mother and immediately got a doctor, Master Francesco, and brought him to Firenzuola where they found Cione in such a bad way that nobody expected him to recover. Yet he did, thanks to the doctor's excellent care and, after having lain there for over a month without moving, was brought to Florence where he was soon as well as ever. I mention this incident, not only on account of the sorrow I felt when I was sitting on that mountainside with my first cousin stretched out on my lap with his head hanging as if he were dead, but also because of something his mother said later to my brother, Piero. Addressing him in a loud voice, in a moment of hysteria or spite or perhaps simply in order to make trouble between us, she said: "You sent Buonaccorso to kill my son and you killed my other son too in your house at Val di Pesa."

I was all the more distressed and hurt by this because of a pouchful of unsealed letters I had taken from Cione's side when he was lying like a dead man in the litter. They were from his cousins, the Mannelli, who had sent them to him at Venice to tell him that when his mother had tried to return to the house where she had lived with her brother, we had struck her and driven her out. When Cione was better I refused to return the letters and told him that I was going to show them to our relatives so that they might learn of the Mannelli's dishonesty. Cione threatened: "If you don't return them I will denounce you and tell how you hit me on the head with your sword, but if you give them back I promise to go on holding my tongue." I guessed that his mother or the Mannelli must have put him up to saying this in the hope of frightening me into returning the letters or even of provoking me into doing him an injury. Thank God I did neither but simply told him, "You did not make up these lies yourself. I know who did and why, but they will neither make me return the letters nor punish you as you deserve. Go off now and slander me to your heart's content.

It's nothing to me for the truth will come out in the end."
Then I took the letters straight over to the house of
Buonaccorso, Rucho Pitti's son, where my brothers were
waiting with our host's son, Luigi, and his grandson, Lionardo, the son of Geppo Pitti, and the wretched Ciro, son
of Lapo Pitti. I told them what Cione had said and showed
them the letters which, after due deliberation, they decided
to keep, telling me to leave the matter in their hands.

About a month later they sent for me. Cione was with
them and, after they had lengthily interceded for him, he
begged my pardon, swearing that he did not remember who
had struck him. This, he explained, was why he had been
foolish enough to repeat what he had heard from trouble-
makers but, since then, God had opened his eyes to the
truth and he was now convinced that he had been stunned by
a kick just as I had said. I pardoned him freely and, many
years later, after repeated entreaties, was even prevailed
upon to forgive his mother. He wanted me to forgive his
cousins, the Mannelli, too, but this I refused to do until,
one Good Friday, fully thirty years afterwards, when so
as to earn grace in the sight of God, I summoned them to
the chapter house in S. Spirito and, with God as our only
mediator, made them an offer of peace which they accepted
in a humble and contrite spirit.

In 1375, being young [twenty-two], inexperienced, and
eager to see something of the world, I joined forces with
Matteo dello Scelto Tinghi, a merchant and a great gambler. We went to Genoa, Pavia, back to Genoa and on to
Nice and then Avignon, which we reached at Christmas
time and where we were seized and thrown into the prison
of the Pope's marshall. When we had been a week in prison,
they had us up for questioning and accused us of being
spies for the Commune of Florence. They produced a letter
to Matteo from a brother of his in Florence telling him
that Florence had instigated Bologna's rebellion against
the Pope. After examining us closely, the court recognized
our innocence but insisted nonetheless on our furnishing a
bail of 3,000 florins lest we leave the city without the

marshal's permission. Matteo found someone to put up
the money and, once we were out of prison, sagely decided
that it would be dangerous to stay on here while our Commune was waging war in the territories of the Papacy. He
concluded that we had better leave town and that if the
merchants who had put up the bail were to lose their money
we would reimburse them. Accordingly, we returned to
Florence with all speed and had not been there long before
news came from Avignon that the Pope had caused all
Florentine citizens to be arrested and their records and
possessions seized. Letters telling the same story came from
all parts of Western Europe where Florentines were being
imprisoned and undone as a result of Pope Gregory's decree. In spite of all this, our Commune kept on with its war
against the priests, who were an unscrupulous lot at the
time—not indeed that I ever met an honest one either before or since![4]

The following year Matteo decided to go to Prussia and
to take me with him. He sent me on ahead, promising to
join me about a month later in either Padua or Venice.
Having visited Padua, Vicenza, and Verona, I came back
to Padua and proceeded from thence to Venice where, when
Matteo arrived, he bought 1,000 ducats worth of saffron.
We set sail from there to Segna in Slavonia and, from
thence, made our way by land to Zagreb and Buda. There,
Matteo sold his saffron at 1,000 ducats' profit, and I fell
seriously ill with a fever and two tumors of the groin.
Matteo left me at Michele Marucci's house at Buda. He
gave Michele twelve ducats to pay my way back to Florence
if I should survive, and promised that on his next visit he
would repay him any expense he might be put to by my illness. Then he went on his way, leaving me alone, in great
discomfort and with no one to look after me.

My bed was a large sack of straw in an alcove, and no
doctor was brought to visit me. There were no women in

---

[4] This war between Florence and the Papacy, called the War of the Eight
Saints, began in July 1375 and ended three years later, in the summer of
1378. The occupant of the Holy See was Pope Gregory XI (1370–1378).

that house either, only a serving lad who was kept busy cooking and waiting on Michele and on a couple of merchants who were staying with him. I came very close to dying. I had been six weeks lying on that sack, with a towel over me in place of a sheet and a shaggy bedcover and a greasy fur coat of my own, when, on St. Martin's Night, a party of Germans gathered in the next room to play the pipes and dance. They stuck their heads in to see who was there and, finding me, forced me into my fur coat and dragged me round and round that room, in spite of all my entreaties, and only let me go when I collapsed from exhaustion. They put me back on my sack then, threw their lined mantles on top of me, and went back to their drinking and dancing. They kept that up all night while I stewed and sweated under that pile of clothes. In the morning, when they came for their mantles, they forced me to dress again and to have a drink with them—which I did willingly enough.

When they were gone, I rested for about an hour before setting out for the house of Guido Baldi from Florence who was master of the royal mint at Buda. He made me very welcome and kept me to dinner, after which we began to gamble. I had only 55 Venetian *soldini* left but I managed to win four florins with these. While we were playing, we were joined by a number of Jews and other Germans who were in the habit of coming over to Bartolomeo's to play. I played with them too and, by the end of the evening, had won 20 gold florins. I came back the next day and won 40 more gold florins, and so on every day for about twenty-five days, by the end of which I had turned my 55 Venetian *soldini* into approximately 1,200 gold florins.[5]

[5] The complexities of European currency in this period have been clarified in a brief but lucid article by P. Spufford in *The Cambridge Economic History of Europe,* III (Cambridge, 1963), 576–602. The most valuable Florentine coin was the gold florin, worth approximately $4.00 at the current price of $35.00 per ounce. Independent of the florin was a monetary system based upon silver, comprising *lire* (pounds), *soldi* (shillings) and *denari* (pence): 12 *denari* to the *soldo,* 20 *soldi* to the *lire.* In 1400, a florin was worth approximately 75 *soldi,* or 3¾ *lire.* Day wages for unskilled laborers

Meanwhile, Michele Marucci kept begging me to stop gambling, saying, "Why don't you buy a number of horses to bring back to Florence? I will take off a few days to accompany you as far as Segna." In the end, I took his advice and bought six fine horses and hired four servants and a page and, when we reached Segna, Michele sold me five of his own horses. I hired a boat from Marseille and stowed the horses on it, but, as ill winds and fortune would have it, we were twenty-four days getting to Venice, and one of the best horses put his shoulder out as we were unloading them. When we reached Padua, I gave one of the horses to Giorgio Bagnesi, who was living there with his wife, Monna Caterina, a daughter of Niccolò Malegonelle and a first cousin of our own.

As the Bolognese were at war at that time, we came back to Florence by the Modena road and, in the mountains above Modena, another good horse was injured and had to be left behind at Pontremoli. I got back here with eight horses and sold six of them for money which I afterwards lost at the gaming tables. And indeed, six months later, what between losses, outlay for clothes, and other expenses, I found myself with no more than 100 florins in hand and two horses.

While I was in these straits, I fell in love with Monna Gemma, the wife of Jacopo, Messer Rinieri Cavicciuli's son, and the daughter of Giovanni Tedaldini. She was staying at a convent outside the city at Pinta. As I happened to be passing by one day, some of her relatives invited me in for refreshments and I accepted. Although there were a number of people present, I managed to have a private word with her and told her very respectfully, "I am entirely yours and I beg you to take pity on me." "Does that mean," she asked me laughing, "that if I were to command you to do something you would obey?" "Try me." "Very well," she said, "go to Rome for love of me." I went home

---

in Florence varied between 7 and 15 *soldi;* a bushel of wheat in times of good harvest cost about 15 *soldi.* A small house might rent for 5 fl. annually; a large palace, for 50 fl.

and two days later, without a word to anyone, took horse and set out with one servant. I went by Siena, Perugia, Todi, Spoleto, Terni, and Narni to Orte where the Florentine League was fighting the Romans. Next, I managed to persuade Messer Bindo Buondelmonti and a group of his men to take me to Rome one night and smuggle me into the house of a secret friend of theirs within the city, Messer Cola Ciencio, who obtained a safeconduct for me for a week. When I had been there six days, he had me taken to a castle belonging to the Orsini, and from there to Orte, whence I returned to Florence by the way I had come. Between going and coming back and the time spent in Rome, the whole trip had taken me a month. When I got home I sent a woman to tell Monna Gemma how I had obeyed her. She sent back word that she had never supposed I would be so mad as to take such a risk on account of a challenge spoken in jest. That was in 1377.

In 1378, after peace had been made with Pope Gregory, disturbances broke out among the Florentine populace.[6] The unskilled workers burned and sacked a number of houses and drove the Priors from the communal palace and with them Luigi Guicciardini who was Standard-bearer of Justice[7] at the time. They then proceeded to take power and to appoint a Standard-bearer of their own choosing, a certain Michele di Lando, who, however, a day or so later, made common cause with the artisans, the Ghibellines and men barred from office, and withdrew all power from the mob.

As a militiaman enrolled under the Nicchio standard,[8] I

---

[6] Pitti is in error; peace was not made with Pope Gregory XI (who died in March 1378) but with his successor, Urban VI, in July 1378. In this paragraph, Pitti is describing the revolt of the Ciompi, a proletarian upheaval which established a regime dominated by artisans and workers in the cloth factories. Created in July, this regime was crushed in late August and replaced by another popular government of artisans and merchants.

[7] The Standard-bearer of Justice was the ninth member of the Signoria. Although his office was considered the most prestigious in the city, the Standard-bearer had no more real power than any of the Priors.

[8] Pitti was a member of the civic militia of his district (*gonfalone*) of Nic-

was on duty in the square when the artisans and their allies were returning after the mob's expulsion. When all the others had quieted down, a stonecutter who was clearly in a murderous mood, kept yelling: "String 'em up! String 'em up!" I walked over and told him to hold his tongue, whereupon he lunged for my chest with the point of his sword. I quickly drew a spear on him and, running it through his leather tunic, killed him on the spot. Several witnesses, who had seen him start the trouble, declared that I had acted in self-defense and that he deserved what he got. No more was said about this at the time.

I went home and, seeing that many Guelf citizens, including some of the best, were being proscribed and banished, resolved to leave the city.[9] I went to Pisa where I was joined by Matteo Tinghi, who had been exiled. Some months later, news reached us here that a number of Guelf citizens were planning to start an insurrection in Florence with the help of a band of proscribed men who were to come in from Siena under the leadership of Messer Luca, Totto da Panzano's son. On hearing this, Giovanni dello Scelto Tinghi and Bernardo di Lippo organized and headed a Pisan contingent of about 200 exiles, proscribed men and sympathizers. I joined this group and, following a prearranged plan, went with them on a certain night at the gate of S. Piero Gattolino. Messer Luca's men were supposed to reach S. Miniato al Monte late the same night so as to sound the tocsin at dawn. This was to be the signal for the conspirators in Florence to arm themselves, take to the streets and open the gate of S. Giorgio to us. Accordingly, our party sent to find out whether Messer Luca was at

chio, one of the four subdivisions of his quarter of S. Spirito. He then lived in the parish of S. Felicità, a short distance from the Pitti palace, which was not built until after his death. Buonaccorso later moved to the parish of S. Felice in Piazza, in the district of Ferze.

[9] The regime which governed Florence from September 1378 to January 1382 was too democratic for Pitti's taste. It had banned several members of prominent aristocratic families, and Pitti decided to throw in his lot with these Guelf exiles. He was convicted of treason and sentenced to death *in absentia*.

S. Miniato. He was not, for the plot in the city had been discovered, and Messer Gregorio Tornaquinci was arrested along with several others from whom the city authorities learned of Messer Luca's plan to come in with his men from S. Maria Impruneta.[10] The *Difensore*[11] was promptly sent out with a number of foot soldiers and fifty cavalry soldiers who, finding Messer Luca's party, captured seven and routed the rest.

Knowing nothing of this and hearing that Messer Luca was not at his post, our group thought we must have come a day too soon. Accordingly, we retreated from Florence towards Possolatico, split into small groups and sought refuge in the houses of friends. I went with Giovanni Tinghi and Bernardo di Lippo to Giovanni Corbizi's house at Pozzolatico where we found shelter for ourselves and for about six horses and twelve foot soldiers. About the hour of nones,[12] a number of fugitives arrived from Florence with the news that Messer Gregorio had been arrested and that the whole city was under martial law. We were still convinced that we had arrived a day early and hopeful that Messer Luca might yet turn up with his men. I therefore took horse as soon as it was dusk and set out with two companions on foot for S. Maria Impruneta to see whether I could find any news of them. At about one in the morning I ran into troops of the *Difensore* who were returning with the seven prisoners and, supposing them to be Messer Luca's contingent, hailed them joyfully. They swiftly surrounded us, turned the points of their lances on us and demanded: "Who are you?" Realizing that I was in a tricky situation, I boldly answered: "Friends." A mounted macebearer stepped forward to ask: "What's your name?" "Buonaccorso." "Let him go," he told the foot soldiers,

---

[10] Impruneta is a town seven miles south of Florence. The church of S. Maria Impruneta houses an old and venerated painting of the Madonna to which miraculous powers were attributed.

[11] The *Difensore* or Defender was a foreign police official, appointed to maintain security and thwart conspiracies in this period of internal crisis.

[12] The ninth hour of the canonical day, or 3:00 P.M.

"he's a friend." But by this time they were all around me and the path was so narrow and bad that I could see no way of turning back. I pressed forward until I had caught up with the cavalry, when the *Difensore* who was with them stopped me and asked: "Who are you?" "I am Buonaccorso Pitti," I told them boldly. "The mace-bearer back there recognized me at once." "What are you up to," he wanted to know, "armed like that at this hour?" For I was wearing a cuirass and carrying a boar spear, and my companions had lances on their shoulders. "I have a quarrel on hand," I told him. "I left Florence at closing time. I am on my way to S. Casciano. I chose this road for fear of being ambushed on the other one and because I heard you were in S. Maria Impruneta." "I believe you," he said, "but just in case you might be one of the men I was sent out to get, I want you to come back to Florence with me." "By all means," I answered, "willingly," and turned my horse around. He demanded my name a second time and asked me the same questions as before, which I answered without flinching. Finally he said, "It doesn't seem right to make you turn back, and yet I am afraid of being blamed if I let you go." "Your Honor," I said, "don't worry about me for I will be happy to return with you." Then he said: "Go, and God be with you." I took leave of him, rode on and, when I was out of sight, doubled back by another route to rejoin my companions and tell them whom I had met. We resolved to lie low until daybreak, when I led them by back roads to Sorbigliano by way of Mezzola where Messer Zanobi gave us lunch. Having brought them a safe distance along the road to Siena, I left them there and turned back towards Pisa. All the roads were guarded and I was in constant danger of being captured, yet I did not begin to be frightened until I was almost at Pisa and already out of danger. Then I was so overcome with fear and exhaustion —not having slept for three nights—that I rested for two days at Pontedera. I heard later in Pisa that Messer Gregorio and the seven prisoners had been beheaded and that I had been tried with a number of others and proscribed.

In 1379 I went to Genoa with Matteo Tinghi. On my return to Pisa, Messer Piero Gambacorta[13] caused myself and a number of other Florentine exiles to be expelled from the city. I went to Siena, stayed there a few months, then came back to Pisa with Giusto della Citerna, another Florentine refugee. Some months after that, in April 1380, Matteo del Ricco Corbizi (whose family live in S. Piero Maggiore's Square in Florence) turned up in Pisa on business. He was a henchman of the clique in power in Florence at the time and was in the habit of insulting Florentine exiles to their faces whenever he met them. He taunted them grossly and openly in private gatherings, in family loggias and on the public square, and one day he tried to make me a butt for his insolence. I told him promptly that if he did not bridle his tongue and give up molesting Florentine exiles and refugees, he would find himself with a bloodied shirt. He began to swagger, and insulted me even more brazenly. I walked away and sent Giusto della Citerna to tell him that in the future I would avoid meeting and speaking with him so as to hear no more of his rudeness, and that as soon as he appeared in a place I would leave it, but that if I heard that he had said anything offensive to my honor, I would make him smart for it. He sent back this answer: "Tell Buonaccorso I don't give a whit for his threats, but that I shall not rest until he and the other Florentine exiles have been put out of Pisa."

A few days later I dined with Matteo Tinghi and, about midnight as we were coming home, ran into Matteo del Ricco. Matteo Tinghi went over to discuss some business matter with him and I, in order to give them time to finish their conversation, moved off to talk to Niccolò, Betto Bardi's son. A few moments later Matteo del Ricco left the other man and began to talk business with Caroccio Carocci. Stopping close to where I was standing, he spoke loudly so that I might hear. "Well Caroccio," said he, "tomorrow I'm off to Florence where I shall repay with deeds a certain person who threatened me with words." Know-

[13] Piero Gambacorta was ruler of Pisa.

ing this was intended for me and that his revenge would fall on my brothers who were still in Florence, I grabbed him by the chest and began to shake him, asking: "Did you want to say something to me?" Before I could stop Niccolò, he gave him a blow on the head which knocked him flat at our feet. A clamor broke out at this and, as I was standing there too dazed to run, the guardsmen arrived and would have arrested me had it not been for Vanni Bonconti, who got between them and me and told me: "run." Niccolò and I went to the home of Messer Gualterotto Lanfranco and told him what had happened. He reassured us, told us not to worry and promised to find us a safe hiding place. That night Matteo died of his wounds. I spent three nights at Messer Gualterotto's, and one at the house of a nephew of his to whom he sent us after Messer Piero had told him that he knew where we were and wanted us handed over.

On the fifth day Caroccio, who was a great friend of Messer Piero's, had dinner with him, and Messer Piero began telling him how much he deplored what had happened, saying: "If I don't have the man who did it arrested, the Florentine government will think I condone the murder of their merchants here in Pisa." Caroccio replied: "Messer Piero, you may be quite sure that there was no premeditation, and that what happened was the victim's own fault for I was with him at the time. We were walking along the street, talking of our own affairs when he stopped in front of Buonaccorso, broke off our conversation and spoke the following words." Caroccio then told Messer Piero exactly what had taken place, reporting Matteo's own words and telling what Niccolò and I had done. He also told about my earlier quarrel with Matteo and of the message I had sent him by Giusto della Citerna and of Matteo's answer, adding that if Matteo had not left the city quickly or died when he did, his persistent taunting of Florentine exiles would have earned him plenty of trouble in other quarters. Messer Gualterotto, who was also at the dinner, was present at this conversation. Messer Piero answered: "Caroccio, you have set my mind at rest. I would not like the two men to be arrested but would be glad if they would leave the city if they are still in it, as I have reason to believe they are, though Messer Gualterotto knows more about this than I do." Then he called one of his men and told him, "Have the guards removed who are on duty at the city gates." Messer Gualterotto came straight to our hiding place, saying, "You are saved," and told us all that had been said.

That night we went back to his house, and the next day we all three took horse and he conducted us to S. Maria in Castello where we dined. He gave me a letter to Duccino d'Arma of Lucca, presenting me to him and begging him to do everything he could for me. This letter was very useful for, only a few days after our arrival in Lucca, a brother of the stonecutter whom I had wounded in self-defense on the square in Florence went to Duccino, in whose employ he was, asking him to let him have enough men to take vengeance on an enemy. He named me and added: "He goes to amuse himself every day in such and such an inn outside the city gates." Duccino, who had received Messer Gualterotto's letter recommending me, told the fellow (whose name was Michele) that if he came back the next day he would give him the men he wanted. Then he came to see me that very evening to tell me what was on foot and to warn me not to stir out of Lucca. I stayed there three days more and then left for Genoa. A few days after my arrival in Genoa, I began to gamble. I had 50 florins to start with and in about a month won about 1,500 more. That was in June 1380.

Giovanni, Bindo della Vitella's son, came to Genoa bringing word from the leading Florentine exiles that King Charles of Naples was expected shortly in Verona and that they were all going to meet there to see what could be done for our cause.[14] I was bound to join them by the terms of an

[14] Charles of Durazzo was one of two Angevin claimants to the Kingdom of Naples. Although thwarted in his attempt to conquer the Kingdom in 1380, he later defeated his rival, Louis of Anjou (uncle of King Charles VI of France), but he died in 1386. Like Florence, the Angevin dynasty was traditionally Guelf, an ally of the Papacy. Florence's aristocratic exiles thus regarded Charles as their natural ally and protector.

undertaking I and several others had signed in Siena, so I bought five excellent horses and a quantity of arms, lent 200 new florins to Niccolò to arm himself and buy a pair of horses, and set off with him for Verona. We found many of the leading exiles there before us and, when we had paid our respects to the King, followed him to the Romagna whither he was bound at the head of a great army of Hungarian, German, and Italian troops.

Bernardo di Lippo, Giovanni di Guerrieri de'Rossi and myself found lodgings in the village that surrounds that Bolognese castle of Sampiero, but we had hardly finished dining there when the stable caught fire. Four of my best horses were so badly burned that I had to leave them behind, and the villeins from the castle came out to kill us. They would probably have succeeded but for a native of Firenzuola who warned us in time to arm ourselves and make a getaway. Some mounted, others on foot, we dragged ourselves to the army camp which was about four miles further on. Later, I bought three new horses in Forlì and a fourth in Rimini.

When we reached Arezzo, the leading Florentines among us persuaded the Albergotti and the Bostoli to hand over the city to the King. On entering the city, Tomasino da Panzano, Messer Bartolomeo da Prato—who had not yet been knighted—and Moscone de' Beccanugi killed Messer Giovanni di Mone, who had been sent as ambassador from Florence to stiffen the Aretines and dissuade them from delivering the city to the King. The King was very distressed by this death and sent word to those responsible for it that they should keep out of his sight.

Leaving Arezzo, we set off for Siena and paused on the way at Staggia. But a few days after we got there, the Hungarians and other mercenaries began to clamor for money, refusing to proceed any further without pay and threatening to take off and abandon the King. He thereupon made a compact with the faction in power in Florence, received 25,000 gold florins from them, and turned back for Arezzo. We refugees, whom he had promised to lead to the very

walls of Florence, bitterly remonstrated with him through
our spokesman, Messer Lapo da Castiglionchio. He replied,
shamefacedly and with tears in his eyes, that he had no
choice but to do as he had done, and that if he once made
good his claim to his kingdom, he would have no rest until
he had reinstated us in our city. A few days later he left
for Rome. Some Florentine exiles followed him, but the
majority had gone through their funds and were obliged to
withdraw from the campaign. I was among these since, of
the 1,500 gold florins I had brought from Genoa in cash
and equipment, only two horses and no money remained.
The rest had been spent or lent to other exiles.

Bernardo di Lippo and I were resolved to go to France.
First we went to Rimini where we borrowed 50 ducats from
Giovanni di Masino dell'Antella. Then, without further
pause, we made for Avignon and Tarascon where we paid
a visit to two other proscribed Florentines, Messer Stoldo
Altoviti and Messer Tommaso Soderini. On leaving them
we went to Paris, but stayed there only a short time. Meanwhile, I had been commissioned by Bernardo di Cino to
play against the Duke of Brabant in Brussels, where he and
many other great gentlemen were beguiling their time with
tournaments, jousting, dancing and the gaming tables. A
few days after reaching Brussels, I had already lost 2,000
gold francs[15] belonging to Bernardo di Cino with whom I
had gone into partnership on the understanding that he was
to supply the money and I my poor skill. I lost it through
making bets of 300 or more florins on each throw of a pair
of dice, having deluded myself that playing for high stakes
would bring me greater profits. On my last night I lost 500
francs which I had borrowed from the Duke and, since all
I had in my lodgings was another 550 gold francs, I left the
tables.

The Duke and a group of gentlemen rose and went into

[15] The gold franc was worth slightly more than the Florentine florin. It con-
tained 3.885 grams of gold to the florin's 3.536. The Venetian ducat, mentioned in the preceding paragraph, was nearly identical in value to the florin.
Its gold content was 3.559 grams.

another room where many ladies and gentlemen were dancing and, as I stood enjoying the spectacle, a young unmar-
ried beauty, the daughter of a great baron, came over to
me and said: "Come and dance, Lombard, don't fret over
your losses for God will surely help you." Then she led me
onto the floor. When I had finished dancing with her, the
Duke called me over and asked, "How much did you lose
this evening?" I told him I had lost all that was left of the
2,000 francs I had brought from Brussels. He said, "I believe you, though if I had lost such a sum I would not be
able to show as cheerful a face as yours. Go back to your
enjoyment now. It can do you nothing but good!"

Next morning I brought the Duke a purse containing 500
gold francs and begged his leave to depart, explaining that
I wanted to seek better fortune elsewhere. He said to me,
"Stay if you like and try to retrieve your losses with these
500 francs. If you lose them you can pay me back some
other time when you are more prosperous." I thanked him
but said I did not want to play any more for a while and
that I had urgent reasons for going to England. He told me
to keep the 500 francs anyway and that I could repay him
if ever I returned and won back the money I had lost.
Then he summoned one of his chancellors and told him to
make out a letter for me, stating that he took an interest
in my welfare, considering me as being attached to his personal service and so forth.

I left Brussels for England where I stayed for about a
month, discussing the terms of a ransom to be paid for Jean
of Brittany as I had been commissioned to do by Bernardo
di Cino. When I had learned the intentions of the Duke of
Lancaster, in whose hands the prisoner was, I returned to
Paris and reported to Bernardo on all I had done in Brussels and England.[16]

On my return to Paris in 1381, I was very short of

[16] Jean of Brittany, or Jean of Blois, had been a prisoner in England for
more than thirty years. He was delivered to the English as hostage for
his father, Charles of Blois, who had been captured in 1345. Jean was finally
released in 1387.

money as a result of my losses in Brussels, especially as, being obliged to repay Bernardo one-quarter of the 2,000 francs I had lost, I gave him the 500 francs which the Duke of Brabant had given me in guise of a loan. That February I went back to Brussels with about 200 gold francs lent me by various people and, while I was there, borrowed another 300 from Bernardo da Varazzano. While I was playing with the Duke and other gentlemen, letters came from Florence with news that the exiles had returned to the city. I did not leave Brussels until the end of Lent, by which time I had saved about 600 gold francs. On my way back through Paris, I bought some fine horses and reached Florence in May 1382.

The following September I went back to Paris and, on St. Catherine's Day in November, was present at a battle which the King of France[17] fought in Flanders near Ypres against the Flemings, or rather against the men of Ghent, whose leader was Philippe van Artevelde. The Flemings had a force of 40,000 armed men and we, on the king's side, were 10,000. The battle was fought on foot at sunrise. What seemed miraculous was that, although at first there was a mist so thick that it was almost like night, when the king, having divided us into three hosts, ordered his standard-bearer to unfurl the oriflamme which is supposed to have been a divine gift to his ancestors, the mist melted away and the two sides were able to see each other by the light of the sun.

The French Commander-in-Chief opened the battle by leading the first of the three French divisions against the Flemings who were drawn up in a single formation. Two hours later it was all over. That one division of Frenchmen had defeated the Flemings. The order was to show no mercy to prisoners and, at the end, the number of Flemings found dead on the field amounted to 27,500. As soon as the battle had been won, we pressed on to Courtrai, a town about the size of Prato, which was taken and sacked and burnt in reprisal for a defeat which the French had suffered

[17] The French king was Charles VI.

near there many years before at the hands of the Flemish when, as one may read in the chronicles of Filippo Villani, a great number of French knights lost their lives.[18] After this, the King set out for Paris at the head of his victorious army. Before telling of the King's arrival in Paris, I will record the events which led up to the battle I have just described.

In 1381 the people of Ghent rebelled against their over-lord, the Count of Flanders, who was the father of the Duchess of Burgundy. They marched in great numbers to Bruges, took the city, deposed the Count, robbed and killed all his officers, and dealt in the same way with all the other Flemish towns which fell into their hands. Their leader was the Philippe van Artevelde whom I mentioned above. As the number of Flemings rebelling against their overlords increased, they sent secret embassies to the populace of Paris and Rouen, urging them to do the like with their own lords, and promising them aid and succor in this undertaking. Accordingly, these two cities rebelled against the King of France. The first insurrection was that of the Paris mob, and was sparked off by a costermonger who, when an official tried to levy a tax on the fruit and vegetables he was selling, began to roar "Down with the *gabelle*!" At this cry, the whole populace rose, ran to the tax-collectors' houses and robbed and murdered them. Then, since the mob was unarmed, one of their number led them to the Châtelet where Bertrand de Guesclin, a former High Constable, had stored 3,000 lead-tipped cudgels in preparation for a battle which was to have been fought against the English. The rabble used axes to break their way into the tower where these cudgels or mallets (in French, *maillets*) were kept and, arming themselves, set forth in all directions to rob the houses of the King's representatives and in many cases to murder them. The *popolo grasso*, or men of substance who in French are called "bourgeois," fearing lest the mob (who were later called *Maillotins* and were of much the

---

[18] The account of the battle of Courtrai (1302) is found in the chronicle of Giovanni Villani, not Filippo; book VIII, ch. 56.

same kidney as the Ciompi in Florence) might rob them too, took arms and managed to subdue them. They then proceeded to take government into their own hands and, together with the *Maillotins,* continued the war against their royal lords.

The King and his household withdrew to the wood of Vincennes and took counsel. To prevent the whole kingdom rising against him, they resolved that the King should summon his barons, knights and equerries to assemble with all their men and prepare to follow wherever he might lead them. Yet, although he urged and commanded their presence as insistently as he could, no more turned up than the 10,000 I mentioned before who were at the battle. After his victory, the saying was borne out whereby nothing succeeds like success. For in the following year, 1383, when he once more summoned his nobles, this time to march against the English who had invaded Flanders—of which I shall tell later on—, he was obeyed by 10,000 knights and more than 16,000 squires who, with their following, amounted to more than 200,000 horsemen, although it is true that there were a number of German lords among them who came out of friendship.

To come back to the King's return to his rebellious city of Paris. He arrived one evening at the Abbey of St. Denis, and the next morning drew up his troops in three divisions as he had done at the battle. On hearing this, the Paris burghers resolved to come before him and beg his pardon. Fully 500 of the most prominent came and, flinging themselves at his feet, begged his forgiveness. The King told them, "Go back to Paris and when I am seated in the place of justice, you will be granted a hearing."

When the King was half a mile from Paris, all the knights, squires and men-at-arms dismounted and formed three divisions. He and his royal household who were in the second division remained on horseback while the rest of us advanced on foot with our helmets on our heads for fear of treachery. We made straight for the great palace where the King dismounted and issued a proclamation commanding every citizen or bourgeois, on pain of the gallows, to deliver up his arms, both defensive and offensive, before sundown, at the royal residence, which is a large and attractive fortress in the city of Paris. This order was obeyed fully and promptly. His next order was that all the chains in the city should be removed, and this too was done. I overheard one of the King's equerries ask him if he might have these chains as a gift and the King, who never refused a request, agreed. At the time the chains did not appear to have much value but later it was known that the equerry had got about 10,000 gold francs for them.

About forty citizens and *Maillotins* who had led the rebellion against the Crown were arrested and beheaded in the square of Les Halles and, after that execution, no further death penalties were pronounced. All the rich burghers were summoned, however, and fines were imposed on each according to his means. Some were assessed as much as 10,000 gold francs and many had to pay 2,000 or more. The King then made these fines payable to the lords and barons who had fought with him in the war. I saw the Duke of Bourbon, to whom the King had allotted 40,000 gold francs' worth of these fines, accept the gift and the following day send for the burghers who were to have paid it and release them from their debt. All the other lords collected their money, however, and the total amounted to about 500,000 francs. After that, the town settled down, and great festivities were organized with jousts, dances and games of chance.

That February, Bernardo di Cino entrusted his nephew Cino with 200 gold francs and with pearls and jewelry to the value of a further 3,000, so that Cino and I might take them to Holland to sell them or play for them with Duke Albert of Bavaria. We got to The Hague and found the Duke, but he would neither buy the jewels nor play for them. The gold francs went in expenses and gambling. By April 1383, we were back in Paris and had returned the jewels to Bernardo.

That year the English landed in France on the border between Flanders and Picardy. They had a fighting force of about 10,000 archers and men-at-arms, and had soon captured several sizeable towns in Flanders. When the King of France heard this, he sent out a summons to his lords and barons and squires and, by August, was in the field with an army of about 200,000 cavalry including 10,000 knights with golden spurs, as I mentioned earlier.

Being eager to partake once more in such great doings, I pooled resources with a man from Lucca and a Sienese. When we had equipped ourselves at our own expense with arms and thirty-six horsemen, we enrolled in the army under the flag and captaincy of the Duke of Burgundy who commanded 20,000 horse. When the army reached Mons, a town of some size in which part of the English forces were garrisoned, the King immediately gave orders for the ground to be levelled so that he might give battle the next day. In the middle of the night, the English tried to escape and, as the townspeople wanted to prevent them, skirmishes broke out in which many were killed. In the end all the English and townsfolk who could fled the city before daybreak. When it was light we closed in on the town, cut off all means of retreat, and entered unopposed. Inside we found most of the houses on fire and heaps of dead English and townsfolk. I saw one cruelly horrifying sight: a woman, who appeared from her clothing to be of good class, was sitting with a two-year-old child in her arms, a three-year-old clinging to her shoulders and a five-year-old holding her hand, by the door of a furiously burning house. She was pulled up and moved some distance away to prevent herself and the children coming to harm but, as soon as she was let go, rushed back in the door of the house, despite the great flames which were billowing from it, and was finally burnt inside with her three children. In the end, the whole town was burnt and destroyed.

We spent the day there, and on the morrow moved off in pursuit of the enemy who kept retreating before us. About the hour of vespers, we reached a big town in which the English had taken refuge, and straightaway set about besieging it from all sides with lighted rockets which we threw in so as to set it on fire. The English defended themselves boldly, firing arrows at our troops which wrought havoc among them and wounded many. We withdrew with great loss and little honor. I lost sight of one of my companions and several of our men who had taken part in the siege and could not find them all night, though in truth I was hardly able to look for them but lay exhausted in a ditch until daybreak.

On Sunday morning the Duke of Brittany, who was at the head of 20,000 horse, made an agreement with the English in the King's name, according to which they were to take whatever they could carry and go back to England. The next day they departed bag and baggage from Flanders. The King thereupon returned to France and to Paris and there discharged all the troops but kept the nobles with him to feast and celebrate.

In February 1384, I went to Brussels and from thence to Holland to visit Duke Albert. On my return, I found that my brother Francesco had come up from Florence and was waiting for me in Paris. I spent all that summer and the winter in Paris, returned to Florence in May 1385, and the following October came back to Paris bringing Bernardo de la Fonte with me. In 1386, I went to Florence in May and in September was back in Paris where I heard that the King of France had led a large army into Flanders and was having a fleet built at Sluys so as to cross over to England. Francesco, Berto, and myself equipped ourselves with arms and horses and set out to join the King, for we were of a mind to follow him to England. When we reached Bruges, I met the man from Lucca who had been my companion in the great army. He was with a compatriot, so the three of us pooled our funds and hired a stout ship with which we sailed to Sluys, where the King and his fleet were getting ready to cross to England. Of the 1,200 ships I saw there, I noticed that 600 were cogs with crow's-nests.

After waiting a fortnight for a favorable wind and sea for the crossing, the King called a meeting of ship owners and experienced sea captains and asked their advice. They told him that in their opinion it was impossible to cross with such a large number of boats. It was already late November. "And," said they, "if we were to meet with rough weather and bad winds while at sea, the ships would collide with each other and many would perish." The King and the Lords of his Council took this advice and we all returned to France.

While we were at Sluys I lent the Count of Savoy about 500 francs to gamble with, and at Bruges another 200 for other purposes, and again at Arras let him have 400 more, and so on all the way to Paris. Thus, by the time we got there, I had helped him out so often that his debts to me amounted to 2,000 gold francs. He spent the winter in Paris and at his departure borrowed a further 1,500 gold francs from me which brought his total debt up to 3,500 francs. At his own suggestion, I sent a man with him to Savoy by whom he was to send back the money. He did not send it but set himself a time limit by which he promised to do so. When this had run out I went to Savoy myself and stayed there more than a month but in the end had to let him extend his deadline by a further six months.

I spent the winter in Paris and went to Holland in Lent to visit Duke Albert. Then I came back to Paris, went to Florence in May 1388, and returned to Paris in September when I brought Francesco Canigiani with me. He had just sold a small farm for 400 gold florins which he deposited with me on the understanding that I was to pay his expenses and give him 100 florins a year for three years. On the same trip, I brought back the steward who was also to have his expenses paid and receive 100 florins a year for three years. I spent the next winter in Paris too and won about 2,000 gold francs. I bought a house for 600 gold florins and in Lent went to Holland and Zeeland to visit Duke Albert and won about 1,500 francs from him and other lords.

I returned to Paris but left it shortly afterwards to follow the King who had set out for Avignon and Toulouse. When I had been a few days on the road, I met Messer

Antonio Porro, the Duke of Milan's delegate to the King. We travelled together and, before we reached Toulouse where the King was staying over Christmas, I had won 1,200 gold francs from him. In St. Sernin I saw the head of St. James in an underground chapel which is said to contain the bodies of six apostles. I saw the burial but not the bodies. They say that wherever the Emperor Charlemagne went, he collected all the saints' bodies he could find and had them sent to Toulouse. This is the basis for the story of the six bodies.

After Christmas we turned back and I met two Florentine ambassadors on the return journey: Messer Filippo Corsini and Messer Cristofano Spini, who were going to Paris to await the King's reply to an embassy with which they had presented him at Lyons on the Rhône.

Without pausing in Paris, I went on to Holland where I won another large sum. After a brief return to Paris, I left again for England in the company of the Count of St. Pol and a number of knights who were going there to take part in some jousts and tournaments. I did not gamble in England but instead gave 500 gold francs to Mariotto Ferrantini and Giovanni di Guerrieri de'Rossi to buy wool and have it sent to me in Florence. I then returned to Paris where I spent the winter. I now possessed 10,000 gold francs between wool, the house, furniture, horses, equipment, and cash, without counting several sizeable sums of money owed me by the Count of Savoy, among others, which amounted to a further 5,000 francs.

My brother Francesco and Francesco Canigiani kept urging me to go back to Florence and leave them in Paris to collect the money that was owing. I decided to do this and, having put Francesco in charge of the house, its furniture, and the sale of some jewels, I gave him 3,000 gold francs in cash, took the good-for-nothing steward with me and set off. I took a round-about route in order to visit the Count of Savoy but could get nothing from him except fresh promises and deadlines.

On reaching Florence I resolved to get married. Since

Guido di Messer Tommaso di Neri del Palagio was the most respected and influential man in the city, I decided to put the matter in his hands and leave the choice of bride up to him, provided he picked her among his own relatives. For I calculated that if I were to become a connection of his and could win his good will, he would be obliged to help me obtain a truce with the Corbizi family. Accordingly, I sent the marriage-broker, Bartolo della Contessa, to tell Guido of my intentions. He sent Bartolo back with the message that he would be happy to have me as a kinsman and was giving the matter thought. A few days later he sent him a second time to say that if I liked I might have the daughter of Luca, son of Piero degli Albizzi, whose mother was a first cousin of his own. I sent back word that I would be very happy and honored and so forth. I was betrothed to her at the end of July 1391 and married her on 12 November of the same year.

One day before my marriage, while I was a member of the Eight on Security,[19] I was in the palace with some companions when lightning struck the palace tower and grounded not far from where I was sitting, so that the fire touched the calves of my legs. When I tried to stand up I collapsed on the ground. I was paralyzed from the knees down and my legs felt as though they were on fire. They removed my stockings which stank of sulphur, for the lightning had missed me by a hairsbreadth. All the flesh of my legs was covered with weals; the skin was bleeding and the hairs were singed. They rubbed my legs which were as cold as those of a dead man and I, thinking I was dying, asked for a priest. Yet half an hour later, I stretched my legs, put on another pair of stockings and walked home on my own two feet.

The wool I had bought in England arrived in two ships before my marriage. The insurance for the consignment unloaded in Genoa was nine per cent of the cost; on the

[19] The Eight on Security (*Otto di Guardia*) was the communal commission for state security.

one that came to Pisa I paid fourteen. When the wool was sold and the money collected, I found that in sixteen months I had made 1,000 gold florins on the venture. I deposited this money with Luigi and Gherardo Canigiani to whom, upon arriving in Florence, I had already entrusted 4,000 gold florins, for which I accepted bills of exchange. This money greatly improved the credit enjoyed by the Canigiani.

Before getting married, I spent about 2,000 gold florins on building and furnishing, and over the years I have had so many restorations and improvements done on this place that, to date, the upkeep of vineyards and plant nurseries alone have cost me more than 2,500 gold florins.

Before I got married, having decided to deal generously with the wretched steward, I gave him 300 gold florins although I only owed him 200. I also entrusted a further 700 to him and yielded to his request that I let him go to Paris to engage in any profitable business he might find. We were to share the proceeds for three years, and if he lost the entire 1,000 gold florins, it was agreed that I was to repay him his own 300. He went to Paris where my brother Francesco set him up in partnership with Luigi, son or Bartolomeo Giovanni, our kinsman. Since Bartolomeo had stayed in my house and worked for me collecting debts (in particular I had sent him several times to Savoy where he twice succeeded in getting 1,000 francs from the Count), I gave him 300 gold francs on my departure from Paris. Having arranged this ill-starred association, Francesco left the pair in Paris and returned to Florence in April. I found him a wife and he got married in June. In September he went back to Paris taking with him our brother Bartolomeo. That December I took Antonio Canigiani with me to Milan and from thence to Pavia and Genoa. Departing on 2 February, I travelled by land and reached Florence on the 5th at the hour of nones.

In March Francesco came back to Florence, leaving Bartolomeo in Paris. He told me that the steward had lost everything except the house and its furnishings, which were worth 1,000 francs in all. Thus, of the 3,000 I had left them, between cash and the value of the house and furniture, they had lost 2,000.

In May I took horse and set out for Avignon and Paris. While I was stopping at an inn in Pavia, I happened to be leaning on a banister at the head of a flight of stairs when a servant, running down, startled a sturdy horse which had been tied to a lower part of the banister. The beast gave it such a tug that the whole thing collapsed and I, falling into the yard below, hit my head against a bin of oats and lost consciousness. No bones were broken and there was no blood. I lay two hours on a bed before I recovered consciousness. When I did, I opened my eyes and asked whether I had broken an arm or leg. Then I became aware of a pain in my head and another in the side on which I had fallen. I asked, "What happened? Who hit me?" For I could not nor ever did remember my fall, although I did remember how the horse had reared when the servant startled him. The Duke of Milan sent all his doctors to me. They drew a lot of blood from several veins, kept me in the dark with the windows closed for nine days, gave me medicines and applied ointments and poultices to my head. On the tenth day I got up and went to thank the Duke.

On taking leave of him, I went to Avignon and Paris where I found Bartolomeo sick. He had contracted about 600 gold francs' worth of debts, since Francesco's departure, between expenses and gambling. I also saw the other two sorry partners in mismanagement who told me, truly or falsely, that they had lost or spent everything. I kept my temper and restored order to my affairs. By the winter of 1393, I had repaid the 600 francs owed by Bartolomeo and given the 300 francs to the steward as I had promised. I also satisfied Luigi and had about 500 gold francs left. I forbade Luigi, the steward, and Bartolomeo to gamble any more before my return and, leaving them in my house, departed for Florence in May 1394.

The following October I left Florence again for Asti, taking my brother Luigi with me, on an embassy from the

Signoria [of Florence] to the Sire de Coucy who was staying there. When I had received a reply, I sent it back to
Florence by Luigi, whom I had brought along for that
purpose. The Sire de Coucy kept me on in Asti until 22
November, when he entrusted me with a secret embassy to
deliver to the King's brother, the Duke of Orleans, whose
equerry I was. The matter was of importance for the
Duke's honor, and urgent since a rival embassy had been
dispatched from Savona a week earlier, whose aim was
contrary to our own and which would be successful if it
reached the Duke in Paris before I did. Accordingly, as
soon as I had received credentials on the 22nd, I set off
from Asti and was in Paris, 450 miles away, on the eve of
St. Andrew's Day [29 November]. On the last two days of
the trip I covered the twenty-four leagues (each league
being about three miles) between Chanceaux and Troyes in
Champagne in a single day, and the thirty-four leagues
(two and one-half miles to the league) between Troyes and
Paris in another. I ruined several horses on that journey
and received compensation for them from the Duke.

In April 1395 the Dukes of Orleans, Berry, Burgundy,
and Bourbon went to Avignon with a number of other lords
to negotiate with Pope Benedict about healing the schism.[20]
I went in the retinue of my lord, the Duke of Orleans.

A month before we left, being owed 600 gold francs by
the Duke of Burgundy for three horses he had had from
me (which had cost me 260 gold florins in Florence), I
found a Burgundy wine merchant from whom I bought 110
casks (or, as they call them there: *cuves*) containing 100
gallons apiece for which I gave 400 in cash and the Duke
of Burgundy's letter of credit for 600 francs. I had the wine
put in two cellars and, as no one would offer me more

[20] Pope Benedict XIII, the Aragonese Pedro de Luna, was the successor of the
Avignon pope, Clement VII, whose election by a group of dissident cardinals
in 1378 had precipitated the Great Schism. The kingdoms of France,
Naples, and Scotland gave their allegiance to Avignon; the remainder of
Latin Europe either adhered to the Roman pope, Urban VI, or remained
neutral.

than 500 francs for it, left it there and told the steward not to sell it for less than 1000. Then I went away with the Duke and while we were in Burgundy, one night in late April, the vines in the area were all nipped by frost. Immediately I sent word to the steward forbidding him to sell any of the wine until I arrived myself. When I got back to Paris I sold 100 casks at fourteen francs cash apiece. I made 400 gold francs on the transaction and kept the remaining casks for my own use. Thus, I was lucky with two of the chanciest of all commodities: horses and wine.

To return to the expedition to Avignon. I saw and heard the dukes appeal to Pope Benedict in public consistory to keep to what he had sworn, signed and sealed with his own seal before his election. This was the promise each cardinal had made before entering the conclave in the interests of restoring unity to our Holy Mother Church, binding himself, if he should be elected pope, to renounce that dignity if and when the College of Cardinals so desired. The Pope replied that he needed time to think over his answer. For three months he held them off with evasive words and resorted to many stratagems to avoid giving them a definite reply. One night, for instance, when the dukes were at Villeneuve-les-Avignon, he had one of the arches of the wooden bridge that spans the Rhône burnt down by secret hirelings in the hope that this would discourage them from coming to Avignon. But, heedless of dangers and discomfort, they crossed the Rhône by ship and continued to press for a reply. Yet, in the end, he told them nothing, but had it publicly announced that he held himself to be the true Pope. He absolved himself of whatever promises he had made before his election, as it was in his power to do, adding that he was ready to seek other means than his own abdication for restoring unity to the Church. After that the lords and dukes returned to Paris.

In September I followed the Duke of Orleans to Mont St. Michel in Normandy, about 150 miles from Paris, where he and the King were making a pilgrimage. When

we arrived we visited the Abbey built on a rock five miles
out to sea, which one can approach by land at low tide.

On his way back to Paris, the King accepted hospitality
from a Norman knight, the Seigneur d'Hambie. The Dukes
of Berry, Bourbon, and Orleans, and the knights and gentlemen who were with them, stayed there for a day and a
night, enjoying lavish entertainment and the company of
many great ladies and beautiful women. I mention this because it was estimated that the Seigneur d'Hambie must
have spent more than 4,000 gold francs that day in the
King's honor, and some said that this was his income for a
whole year. The King brought him back to Paris and
showered him with rich gifts of horses, jewels and cash to
the value of about 10,000 gold francs, so that he paid
generously for the hospitality he had received. And certainly that feast was an extraordinary and wonderful sight
to have seen!

Next day after dinner I accompanied the Duke of Orleans to the house of one of the King's equerries whose
name was Siferval. A number of gentlemen who had dined
there were sitting at the gaming tables when we came in.
The Duke joined them and told me that I should play too,
and to draw on the sum of 400 francs which I had brought
for the two of us. When it was my turn to throw the dice I
deliberately kept challenging the Viscount de Monlev,[21] a
big gambler and a great gentleman who enjoyed an annual
income of over 30,000 francs. Some talk was aroused by
the fact that I won twelve times in a row both on his throws
and on my own. He had drunk a lot of wine, and growing
heated by the game, began to insult me saying: "Hey, Lombard! Are you going to go on winning all night, you
damned cheat? Are you, you sod, you bugger?" I said, "My
Lord, from consideration for His Grace the Duke, try to be
civil!" Then I put down another stake. I won it. At this he
flew into a rage and repeated his foul insults, winding up:
"And this is no lie!" "It is, my Lord!" I answered

[21] Probably Robert de Béthune, Viscount of Meaux.

promptly. He stretched out his hand, pulled the hat from my head and tried to hit me, but I leaped aside, crying: "I am not one to let myself be struck when I am armed," and put my hand to the rapier I wore at my side. He yelled: "I have never been given the lie and now I shall have to kill you!" The Duke told me in a whisper that I should leave things to him and go and wait for him in his room. I left and, when I had gone about a hundred yards from the house, heard someone running behind me. I turned and, by the light from the torches of a group of courtiers who happened to be passing by at that moment, saw and recognized a bastard of the Viscount de Monlev with a naked dagger in his hand. I drew my rapier, crying: "Bastard, go back to your father and tell him you could not find me!" He looked around and, seeing that none of his followers were coming, decided to do as I said. My behavior was wisely reported by the courtiers who had witnessed it and was greatly commended, for the bastard was only eighteen and a weakling whom I might easily have injured.

I went to the Duke's room, and shortly afterwards he entered in a state of great agitation but would say nothing to me. He told one of his grooms, "Go to the Viscount's house and tell him that before I go to sleep I want to know whether he is going to do what I asked." The groom went and came back with the message that the Viscount had not changed his mind. Then the Duke told me, "Don't go out of this house without me, for I will protect you in spite of him and the matter will bring him little honor!"

The next morning we took horse and set out after the King, who had left town. We caught up with him at an abbey where he had stopped for lunch, and the Duke told him of what had happened the night before, begging his permission to protect his dependents, among whom he counted me. The King replied: "The Viscount acted and spoke wrongly and Buonaccorso could not, without loss of honor, do less than answer him. However, I do not want the matter to go any further." Then he summoned the Dukes of Berry and Bourbon and a number of other great lords and told them with an angry look: "Send for the Viscount and tell him that before he leaves this room I want him to satisfy my brother on the matter concerning himself and Buonaccorso." The Viscount came and, in the presence of the King and all the company, the Duke of Berry told him what the King desired. The Viscount turned to the Duke of Orleans, saying: "My Lord, I am distressed that you should side with a Lombard against myself who am a relative and humble servant of your own. There was no need to talk of the matter to the King for I am ever at your orders. If I refused your request last night, it was because I did not believe you to be serious. Now that I see you are, I am willing to overlook the fact that Buonaccorso gave me the lie in your presence last night!" The Duke answered: "You had first spoken to him in such a way in my presence that if he had remained silent I would have considered him worthy of contempt!"

Then I, who was standing nearby and had heard what the King and everyone else had said, came forward and bowed to the Duke of Berry who told me, "His Majesty has heard of the exchange you had last night with the Viscount and is greatly displeased. You, Buonaccorso, were certainly overly bold to give the lie to a lord who is related to ourselves and who has the right to challenge and fight any lord or prince, be they ever so great, with the sole exception of those whose armorial bearings are the lilies of France. But since His Majesty the King is disposed to clemency and does not want this matter to go any further, he desires the Viscount to pardon you and be friendly with you as before. Therefore you, Buonaccorso, beg the Viscount's pardon." "I beg your pardon if I have done something to offend you." He answered, "Since it is the King's pleasure and that of my Lord his brother, I would pardon you even if you had disfigured my face, and so I pardon you and moreover beg your pardon and desire to be at peace with you."

When we returned to Paris I invited the Dukes of Bourbon and Orleans to dine in my house. They came and brought with them the Sire de Coucy and the Viscount and many other barons and knights. They were served such excellent viands and savories that they spoke of it afterwards with great enthusiasm to other lords and even before the King. That dinner cost me 200 francs. My guests had only one complaint, which was that I refused to gamble that night although the play was skillful and for high stakes— for I had invited Bernardo, son of Cino de' Nobili, who was the most stylish and daring gamester ever seen.

1396. That spring I resolved to go back to Florence and, since I did not intend returning to Paris nor to ever play again, sold my house for 1,000 francs—it had cost me 600 —to Bernardo di Cino. I let the steward have the furnishings cheaply and, on the eve of my departure, went to take leave of the King and Queen. The Queen[22] told me not to leave without seeing her again, but to wait until she sent for me. A few days later she did so. Her brother, Duke Ludwig, was with her and, after some affable conversation, she begged me to endeavor to persuade the Commune of Florence to send ambassadors to the King soliciting his alliance against the Duke of Milan, adding that she was sure the King would comply. Then she gave me credentials to present to the Signoria of Florence.

I reached Florence towards the end of May 1396 when, having first revealed my mission in private to some of the more judicious members of the two Colleges, I formally presented my embassy to the Signoria. It turned out that Messer Maso degli Albizzi had already been dispatched on an embassy to the King of France with a request for troops and a captain to be furnished in case of need and at our expense. After a number of consultations and discussions, it was decided that I should return to Paris with a mandate authorizing Messer Maso and myself to conclude

[22] Charles VI's queen was Isabella of Bavaria; her brother Ludwig was Duke of Bavaria. She sought revenge against Giangaleazzo Visconti for the murder—rumored but not proved—of his uncle and her grandfather, Bernabò Visconti, in 1385.

an alliance with the French King.[23] I left on 20 July and received a salary of four florins a day.

Before leaving, I bought from Migliore di Giunta two farms at Montughi in the parish of the Badia of Fiesole. I gave 700 gold florins for them and paid all the tax. I want to note here too that in 1391 I bought a farm from Luigi di Buonaccorso di Rucco Pitti for 700 gold florins and paid the whole tax. The name of this farm is Bossoli and it lies below Sorbigliano in Val di Pesa. That same year I paid 400 gold florins to Andrea Belincini for a house which my brother Francesco had mortgaged to his brother Niccolò, and another 300 gold florins to Lisabetta the daughter of Cione di Buonaccorso Pitti.

I left Florence on 20 July 1396 and went to Paris via Lombardy, which was risky because of my embassy from the Signoria. I had with me Vanni Stefani the notary attached to our delegation, and had great trouble getting him to Paris as he was unused to riding and had never been out of Florence before. On reaching Paris, I found that Messer Maso had already obtained what he wanted from the King. I showed him the mandate from the Signoria, and we proceeded to carry it into effect with all dispatch. By September we had concluded the alliance with the King of France. My role in this matter gave offense to the Duke of Orleans who had previously been very well disposed towards me. The Duke of Milan was his father-in-law and before the conclusion of the alliance he sent an equerry to me in secret—a certain Bonifazio del Madruccio—asking me to refrain, out of friendship for him, from any act of hostility towards his father-in-law and threatening me in veiled terms. I did not, however, let this affect my zeal or patriotism, but persevered in my endeavors.

We left Paris and took the road to Avignon, intending

---

[23] Florence's first war with Giangaleazzo began in 1390 and ended in 1392. Hostilities broke out again in early 1396, which prompted the Commune's efforts to ally with France. The alliance was signed on 29 September 1396. A truce in May 1398 ended this phase of the struggle.

to board ship at Porto Pisano but in the end, by the grace of God and thanks to the advice of Cardinal Corsini[24] from Florence, we changed our minds and continued our journey overland. The ship we were to have taken was wrecked at sea and all aboard were drowned including, among other Florentine merchants, Giovanni, son of Ser Landi Fortini. We left Avignon on St. Martin's Day and on reaching Asti sent a courier to the Duke of Milan to ask him for a safe-conduct. But then, finding that rumors about our embassy had spread, we left on the third day before dawn and by taking the route through Genoa avoided passing through the Duke's territory. We got to Genoa and Portovenere where we were held up for several days by bad weather and finally reached Florence on Christmas Day. It had taken us forty-six days to come south from Avignon.

As soon as we arrived, ambassadors were chosen to go back to France. These were Messer Vanni Castellani, the lawyer Messer Filippo Corsini, and myself. The Signoria commanded me to press on ahead with all speed, and so I left on 15 January and went by way of Friuli and Germany. The journey took me thirty-four days, during which I was constantly in the snow except when I was indoors. I spent five days at the foot of a mountain called the Arlberg and finally got through by using shovelers and oxen to clear a way for me through the snow. I traveled via Constance, Basel, Langres, and finally reached Paris where I discovered that the King was seriously ill and that news had just come of the French defeat in Turkey: two reasons which made it impossible for me to do much before the arrival of Messer Vanni Castellani and Messer Filippo Corsini. They came bringing with them my brother Luigi. We waited four months, during which time no one in Paris had a mind for anything except the funerals of the royal princes

[24] Cardinal Piero Corsini was an adherent of the Avignon pope, even though his native city recognized the Roman pope as the legitimate head of the church.

and gentlemen killed in Turkey and for the malady and madness of the King who had had to be locked up.[25]

On his recovery he summoned his Council. We presented ourselves immediately and our spokesman, Messer Filippo, set forth our embassy. He did this with such noble eloquence that all the Lords of the Council and many who did not belong to it begged for a copy of his speech and we, at the request of the King himself, provided a written text. The tenor of it was that we wanted the King to honor the obligations he had contracted on concluding our alliance. He replied that he would answer us on another occasion. We repeated our petition several times and each time he answered very amiably that he would do his duty by us and held us off with these words for over two months.

It occurred to me finally, and Messer Vanni and Messer Filippo agreed with me, that since neither the King nor the Dukes knew Latin—apart from the Duke of Orleans who was on the side of the Duke of Milan—and since Messer Filippo had repeatedly and pressingly presented his suit in Latin without obtaining any satisfaction, it was highly probable that the Chancellor and other prelates who understood him had not been translating the true meaning of Messer Filippo's speeches for the King. We resolved accordingly that the next time we addressed him in Council, I should be spokesman and press our suit in French. I did this and spoke very pithily to the effect that our Commune and Signoria, his devoted allies, etc., hoped it would please His Majesty to keep faith with the promises that had been made in his name at the time of signing the alliance, etc. When I came to the words "keep faith," I saw him wince and change color. We then left the audience room. We heard later that as soon as we had gone out the King had asked: "What promises are these which I am being asked

[25] Charles VI's fits of insanity became increasingly frequent as his reign progressed. Undoubtedly contributing to this attack was the news of the disaster at Nicopolis in the Balkans (September 1396), where a French crusading force was massacred by a Turkish army.

to keep? Bring the documents!" When he saw what he had
promised, he admonished the Chancellor and the others
who had understood Messer Filippo's speeches and had
not properly explained to him the passage about his promises which I had just made clear.

He had us called in and the Chancellor addressed us. He
conveyed the King's apologies for not answering and complying sooner with our request. Speaking very courteously,
he explained that the reasons for the delay were to be found
in the King's malady and the death of his relatives in
Turkey, but that the King meant to do his duty by us. When
he had finished speaking, the King said, "I confirm everything my Chancellor has told you, and let neither you nor
anyone think that I renege on my promises!" Then, turning to me, he said: "Buonaccorso, you who so forcefully
reminded me of my obligations, do not let this happen a
second time for there was never and never will be any need
to ask me to honor my word! I am well aware that I am
bound by it. I will never break it and I do not remember
anyone but you ever asking me such a thing!" I rose from
my seat and throwing myself on my knees, said, "Sacred
Majesty, if I have offended you, I humbly beg your pardon.
It was our need, on seeing you did not understand Messer
Filippo who had repeatedly asked you the same thing,
which spurred me to speak to you the way I did." Then the
Duke of Burgundy intervened, saying, "Sire, the Florentines
are such devoted servants of Your Majesty's that they have
taken the liberty of speaking to you without formality."
The King said he was satisfied but remarked with a smile,
"Buonaccorso must make amends to me!"

We left the audience room. A few days later the King
and Council elected a captain: Bernard, Count of Armagnac. He was to assemble an army of 1,000 lances with five
horse for each lance and bring it to Lombardy, where he
was to put himself at the disposal of our alliance. He was
to receive six months' pay from the King. The Count accepted, and we went to see him and congratulated him,
begging him not to lose time. He told us that he intended

to come with 10,000 horse and to pitch camp as close as possible to the Duke of Milan's forces. We encouraged this plan and a day or so later Messer Vanni left with the news for Florence. Messer Filippo and I stayed on to hasten the Count's departure. But, as the Duke of Orleans did everything he could to prevent it, the Count had to wait another month before getting the money for the men's pay. When he had it, he sent for us and said, "I want to go to my own province to recruit 10,000 cavalry, men who got their training in the front line of battle, not in the taverns of Paris. I will bring them as far as Avignon by mid-April, but will not be able to get such a large force any further without support from your Commune and its allies. Therefore, one of you had better go on to Florence and tell them there that if they want me to press forward with my army, I will need 10,000 florins for the six months I will be in enemy territory. If they agree to this I will go to Asti with my men, where I shall expect to find 25,000 florins ready for me. If they do not agree, I shall not go myself but will send a competent captain with the number of men whom the King is disposed to pay. Let me know whether the answer is 'yes' or 'no' at Avignon in April."

We resolved that I should go. I went by Burgundy, Germany and the Friuli as far as Treviso, where I heard that Florentine ambassadors were at a meeting in Venice with the Lord of Padua and other allied ambassadors. I hired two mounts and, sending all my own horses and servants except for one to Padua, went to Venice where I contacted our ambassadors and told them my news. They immediately discussed it with the other legates, who all agreed to contribute to the 10,000 florins. Our ambassadors urged me to make haste to report on this new development in Florence and also wrote letters themselves.

I left Venice on 22 March at nine o'clock, landed at Mestre and reached Padua at two in the morning. On the morning of the 23rd, I took two good horses belonging to the Lord of Padua and, without pausing to eat or drink, reached Ferrara at eight in the evening. Here I changed

horses for two belonging to the Marquis and pressed on to
S. Giorgio, about ten miles outside Bologna. I slept there
and the next morning was at Bologna before sunrise and
hired two nags with which I rode on to Scarperia, where I
slept, and went on from there to Florence, which I reached
at the hour of terce[26] on 25 March. Thus in two days and a
few hours I rode from Padua to Florence, having already
ridden from Paris to Padua in sixteen days.

I reported everything to the Signoria and to the Ten on
War[27] who promptly resolved to send Berto Castellani to
Avignon to tell the Count of Armagnac that he would find
25,000 florins waiting for him in Asti and that everything
he had asked for would be done. Some days after Berto's
departure, I received a letter from the Count telling me that
he needed the money in Avignon. I showed the letter to the
Ten, who broke with him forthwith and sent word to our
ambassadors in Venice to sign an agreement with the Venetians binding ourselves to follow their lead in making peace
or war with the Duke of Milan. This brought little honor
to our Commune, for shortly afterwards came the truce
and the false, brief, and ill-starred peace with the Duke of
Milan.

Meanwhile, the Count of Armagnac had reached Avignon with an army of 10,000 cavalry and was waiting for
100,000 francs (equal to 90,000 gold scudos) to come from
Paris. These had already got as far as Pont-Saint-Esprit,
when the Duke of Orleans (who had already held them up
as long as he could by his allegations in the King's Council
that he knew for a fact that our coalition was preparing to
make peace with the Duke of Milan) received letters from
the said Duke telling him of the truce and the projected
peace. The Duke showed the letters—which had taken a

---

[26] The third hour of the canonical day, or 9:00 A.M.

[27] The Ten on War (*Dieci di Balìa*) was a magistracy selected for a term
of six months, to direct the Commune's military operations. It was a special
commission, appointed only during times of war or impending war. This
magistracy had great authority, assuming many of the functions and respon-
sibilities of the Signoria in peacetime.

mere week to get from Pavia to Paris—to the King and Council, who promptly dispatched a courier after the bearer of the 9,000 scudos countermanding his orders to pay them to the Count. This courier caught up with the first messenger at Point-Saint-Esprit, and the outcome was that the Count of Armagnac went back to his lands in a fury both with us and with the Lords of France who had involved him in enormous losses and expense. The King of France was offended, too, since we had made peace without consulting him, while we were indignant with him because his delays had let us in for great risk, heavy outlay, and little honor.

In 1398 my name was drawn from the pouch (made up in 1382) and on 15 September I entered the College of the Twelve Good Men. On the 30th of the following October, we conducted a scrutiny of names to be put in a pouch which was being made up for the office of Podestà of Pistoia. I was utterly opposed to this measure and spoke and voted against it with all my might, for it seemed to me to be an encroachment on the freedoms which had been promised to the people of Pistoia. On 2 December, we began the general scrutiny, and the custodians of the purses were Lorenzo d'Agnolo, a farrier, Nastagio Bucelli, Francesco, son of Neri Ardinghelli, and Andrea, son of Messer Ugo della Stufa. My scrutators were Gherardo Canigiani and Gherardo Bovongniuoli.[28]

On 1 July 1399, I was selected as one of the priors. My colleagues were Giovanni di Messer Donato Barbadori, Stefano Raffacani, Deo Bentacordi, Michele Altoviti, An-

[28] Pitti is here describing the scrutiny, the method by which most communal offices were filled. In the general scrutiny held in December 1398, citizens were nominated for the Commune's chief executive offices: the Priorate, the Sixteen Standard-bearers of the Militia Companies, and the Twelve Good Men. Those who received a two-thirds vote (by a special commission appointed for this purpose) were declared eligible for all of these offices, and their names were written on paper slips and placed in special pouches or borse. It was from one of these pouches, filled in 1382, that Pitti's name was drawn for the office of the Twelve, a post which he occupied from 15 September to 15 December 1398.

tonio di Durante, Simone Biffoli and Attaviano di Ser Tino Della Casa. The Standard-bearer of Justice and Giovanni di Giovanni Aldobrandini. During my tenure in the Signoria, news came that King Ladislaus, having taken Naples, had recovered the whole kingdom, and that King Louis had gone back to France.[29] The citizenry was eager to celebrate this with a great holiday and for two weeks I argued against our holding a public celebration since we were officially still allies of the King of France. I advised that instead an embassy should be sent to King Ladislaus bringing him our encouragement and a secret gift of up to 10,000 florins, which ought to please him more than the 6,000 I estimated we would spend on a public holiday. Yet in the end the holiday was held with ringing of the palace bells and three days of jousting, bonfires, and tournaments.

During my term in the Signoria, a great novelty was seen throughout Italy when people of all conditions began to don white linen robes with cowls covering their heads and faces, and throng the roads, singing and begging God for grace and mercy. While this was going on in Florence someone raised the cry: "Open the Stinche prison and free the prisoners!" By God's grace the danger of armed riots was averted, though it was a near thing. In the end everything turned out well, for the pilgrims brought about many reconciliations between citizens. Our family, the Pitti, made peace with Antonio and Geri di Giovanni Corbizi, the nephews of Matteo del Ricco whom I had killed in Pisa, and with Matteo di Paolo Corbizi. The compact was notarized by Antonio di Ser Chello.

On 22 September I took office as Captain of Pistoia[30]

[29] Ladislaus, the son of Charles III of Durazzo, inherited the Kingdom of Naples upon his father's death in 1386. Louis II, Duke of Anjou, maintained his claim to Naples after his father died in 1384. His sporadic efforts to conquer the Kingdom kept southern Italy in turmoil until his death in 1417.

[30] This was the first of several offices in the Florentine dominion which Pitti filled. The Pistoian captaincy, the chief executive office of that important city twenty miles northwest of Florence, combined military, judicial and administrative functions. Pitti was responsible for internal and external

where, in the course of my duties, I arrested a public thief. The Signoria of Florence promptly sent a mounted guardsman with a written order requiring me to consign the thief to him so that he might bring him to the Podestà in Florence. Instead of complying with this order, I wrote to the Signoria begging them to respect the rights of the people of Pistoia. They sent back a message to the effect that, if I did not hand the thief over at once, they would inflict such punishment on me as would be a perpetual example to all who might be tempted to disobey them. Yet I still held out and wrote asking my brothers to take counsel with our friends and relatives and, if they were in agreement, to intercede with the Signoria on my behalf, begging them to allow me to administer justice and keep faith with the oaths I had sworn on entering office in Pistoia. My brothers accordingly went before the Signoria with a deputation of friends and relatives and, flinging themselves at their feet, pleaded my case. As soon as they had left the audience chamber, the speaker, Giovanni di Tignosino Bellandi, put to the vote a motion condemning me to twenty years banishment. Twenty-three black beans[31] were cast—another two would have carried it. My brothers were called back, told what had happened and warned that if I failed to deliver up the thief within three days, the motion would be put to the vote again and as many more times as would be necessary to pass it. My brothers informed me of all this and urged me, in the name of our friends and family, to yield.

I called a meeting of the Priors and leading citizens of Pistoia and told them the whole story, letting them read the letters I had received. I told them it was up to them to decide what they wanted me to do and that, for my part, I was ready to suffer exile and other trials in defense of their

security, and was also a judge with authority to inflict capital punishment. His selection to this prestigious office, and his independent behavior while exercising it, are indications of his high political status in Florence.

[31] Black and white beans were used as tallies in balloting. A black bean signified a vote in favor of a proposition; a white bean indicated a negative vote.

rights, and would not violate these without their consent. After consulting together for a while, they told me with tears and sighs, that they would always be grateful for what I had done but that, as the Signoria was clearly determined to override their rights, any further resistance on my part could only lead to danger for me and possibly greater harm for themselves. And thus the lesser evil seemed to be that I should send the thief to Florence—which I did.

In 1400 I set out for Savoy to try and collect the accursed money I had lent the Count. On reaching Padua, however, I found, when I had informed the local lord of my errand, that I could not cross into Savoy without written authorization from the Duke of Milan. The Duke, I was told, had issued orders to this effect and had received promises of obedience from the lords whose territories I would have to cross. I resolved to turn back and was not sorry to do so, for it was with the greatest reluctance that I had left my brothers and their families in Sorbigliano, where they had taken refuge from the plague then raging in Florence.

I went to Bologna and from there dispatched horses and muleteers with letters to my brothers telling them to join me with our families. They came and, about a week after their arrival, I rented the Bianchi family palace and gardens about a mile outside Bologna and installed my brothers and their families there, with the exception of Piero who stayed with his family in Montughi. By God's grace we were all safe and sound but for a son who was born to me there and died. Between ourselves, our immediate families and other relatives who came for visits, there were never less than twenty-five people staying in the house. We spent about four months there and our expenses by the time we got back to Florence amounted to 480 florins.

That year, while many citizens were away in Bologna for fear of the plague, the political exiles seized the opportunity to foment a conspiracy against our government among some young men captained by Salvestro di Messer Rosso de' Ricci. The plotters were betrayed by Salvestro di Messer Filippo

Cavicciuli. Samminiato d'Ugucciozo de' Ricci and a member of the Davizi family were sent to the block. Many were exiled; many more were pardoned and calm returned to the city.

I was elected ambassador that year and sent to Germany to the newly elected emperor, Rupert, Duke of Bavaria and Count Palatine. My mission was, first of all, to convey our congratulations on his election; secondly, to entreat him to come to Rome for his coronation; thirdly, to persuade him to defend his imperial prerogatives, in particular those usurped by the Duke of Milan; fourthly, to assure him that, if he were to engage to do this that very year—1401—we would give him 100,000 gold florins; fifthly, to solicit his confirmation of the imperial privileges delegated to ourselves and to extend our vicariate to Arezzo, Montepulciano and all the other imperial cities then in our possession.[32]

On 15 March I left Florence in the company of Ser Pero da S. Miniato and, following the instructions I had received, went through Padua where I informed the Lord of Padua of my mission. He sent an ambassador of his own with us whose name was Dorde. We went by way of Friuli, Salzburg, Munich, and Ingolstadt to Hamburg, where we found the Emperor. I presented the compliments and homage of our Commune and told him that I was ready to expound my embassy either publicly or for his private ear, whenever and however it should best please himself. He received us eagerly and said he would hear our message later. Meanwhile we were lodged at his expense in a very fine house where we were waited on by his own servants.

On the second day he sent for us and asked me to deliver my message in the presence of about eight members of his

[32] In theory, Florence was subject to the Holy Roman Emperor, although in fact the Commune was independent. While permitting no imperial interference in her affairs, foreign or domestic, the Commune occasionally was willing to pay for the grant of an imperial vicariate, a license for self-government.

Council. I did so but, although I alluded to the gift of money our Commune might be prepared to make, I did not name a figure. The Emperor said he would appoint delegates to negotiate with us and so he did. These in the course of our negotiations questioned us about the amount our Commune was likely to donate. I asked them how much would seem adequate to them and they replied that if the Emperor were to come to Italy that year he would need 500,000 florins from us. I said I wanted to reply to this point in the Emperor's own presence. He received us and I said: "Your Majesty, your delegates have asked for a sum which seems so extraordinarily high to us that we can only conclude this request to be a polite way of refusing to come to Italy, for you must surely know that such an amount is beyond the means of our Commune." He said I was right in thinking he did not want to come that year for he had not the money to do so. The 300,000 florins he had received before his election had all gone to pay for the two sessions of the Diet he had held since then. Another year when he had more money he would not ask us for so much, but if we wanted him to come that year he would be obliged to let us bear most of the expense.

We earnestly exhorted him to come and I finally revealed the figure agreed upon by our government. He replied that, if that was the extent of my message, I should write to Florence what he had told me—that he had no money. I did so and sent duplicate letters by my own couriers. I got a reply to the effect that I should try to convince him by pointing out that the situation at the moment was propitious but might well change if he were to delay. I was authorized to offer him up to 200,000 florins and the promise that once he was in Italy we would do everything in our power to help him. After receiving this, we had several prolonged audiences with His Majesty, during which I kept increasing the amount of our offer until finally, having reached the limit I had been set, I had to tell him that was as high as we could go. He said then that he would summon his Electors and barons to Nuremberg, which was a two-day journey

from where we were, and deliberate with them before giving us a reply.

While we were still waiting for the answer from Florence, we dined with him in one of his gardens and I, noticing that he took no precautions against poison, said,
"Your Highness, you don't seem to realize the villainy of
the Duke of Milan. If you did, you would be more careful
of your safety, for you may be sure that when he hears you
are resolved to cross into Italy, he will make every effort to
have you murdered by poison or by steel." At this he grew
very perturbed and made the sign of the cross, saying,
"Could he be so villainous as to try to kill me before I
have declared war on him or he on me? I find this hard to
believe, yet I will take your advice and be more careful."
And so he did, and one result of the suspicion I had aroused
in him was that whenever he saw a stranger he immediately
inquired who he was and what was his business.

Once, when he and we, who were with him all the time,
were staying for the hunting in a fine castle he owned, a
short day's ride from Hamburg, he stepped out one morning to hear mass and, noticing a man dressed as a courier,
summoned and questioned him. The man said he was on his
way to Venice and had come to have a look at the Emperor
so as to be able to give an account of him when he got there.
The Emperor told one of his knights to take the man to
his room and keep him there until after mass. When mass
was over, the man confessed that he had come from Pavia
with a letter for the Emperor's physician from Master
Piero da Tosignano, the physician of the Duke of Milan,
and that he had brought such letters before. The Emperor
read the letter and sent for his physician, whose name was
Master Herman and who was a former pupil of Master
Piero da Tosignano. And in short the physician confessed
that he was to have poisoned him and was to have received
15,000 ducats for the deed, 5,000 to be paid in Mainz and
the other 10,000 in Venice. When we left for Hamburg,
the courier and the physician were brought along under
heavy guard. As we were riding back, the Emperor called

for me and told me what he had discovered, saying: "Your
warning saved my life."

We went from there to Nuremberg where we were
joined by the Archbishops of Cologne and Mainz, both of
whom were Grand Electors, and by a number of other
barons to whom the Emperor forthwith related his dis-
covery. He also sent for the city authorities and told them
the story, saying that as the incident involved himself he
did not wish to be the judge but would hand the physician
over to them so that they might question him and deal
with him as they thought just. They brought the man to
their palace for interrogation and, finding that he had
truly intended to poison the Emperor, decreed that he
should be dragged to the place of justice and that his legs,
arms, and back should be broken and he should be bound
to a cart wheel and raised on a pole and left there until he
died. And so it was done.

After this the Emperor held council. The question under
debate was whether he should go to Rome for his coronation, but as too many councilors were missing for a decision
to be reached, he resolved to go to Mainz and assemble a
quorum there, which he did. After prolonged discussions
it was agreed that if he came to Lombardy with his army
and spent the whole month of September there we would
give his delegate at Venice 50,000 florins outright and a
further 150,000 in installments. After that we followed him
ten German miles south to Heidelberg, whither he had
summoned a number of great merchants who had engaged
to lend him 50,000 ducats in Augsburg where his army was
to assemble. The merchants were to get back this money
from us in Venice as soon as the Emperor reached Lombardy. But when the merchants came they said they could
not keep their promise because other merchants from whom
they had hoped to get the cash had absolutely refused it
when they heard what it was for. Having failed to cajole
or frighten them into keeping their promises, the Emperor
finally sent for us and told us what had happened. He was

almost in tears. "I shall be dishonored," said he, "on their account. Relying on the promises they made me in Mainz, I sent out a summons to my lords and barons and men-at-arms, bidding them assemble at Augsburg in August so as to accompany me to Lombardy. But see how the merchants have failed me! Therefore I entreat you, Buonaccorso, go, make haste and tell those devoted sons of mine, the Florentine Signoria, what has happened and implore them to save my honor and their own interests if they want me to be in Lombardy at the appointed time. Tell them that if I am to leave Augsburg I must have an advance of at least 25,000 gold ducats on the promised sum."

I was extremely reluctant to make the journey to Florence myself and pointed out that it would be both quicker and safer to send couriers with duplicate letters. The Emperor, however, would not hear of this, so in the end I gave in, fearing that if I did not we would never get him to Lombardy that year. I left Heidelberg on 18 July and in twelve days had covered the 500-mile journey between there and Padua. The Lord of Padua was so astonished at my speed that he would not have believed me but for a letter which I brought him from the Emperor. I had a four-day fever on me when I left Padua which got so bad I could not ride but had to lie up for a day at Rovigo. The day after that I took a boat which brought me by various canals to the Po and from there to Francolino, where I again took horse and managed to get as far as the Poggio di Messer Eghano where I spent the night. Two and a half days later, though still feverish, I was back in Florence where I made my report to the Signoria, their Colleges and a special council. After that I went home and a few days later had got over my fever and was as well as ever.

The Signoria and the Ten on War resolved that Andrea di Neri Vettori (who was later dubbed a knight) and I should go to Augsburg and tell the Emperor that as soon as he had drawn up a deed stating the terms and clauses of our agreement he might send to Venice for the 50,000

ducats which would be there in the keeping of their commissioner, Giovanni di Bicci de' Medici.[33] We set out from
Florence on 15 August in the company of Giovanni di Bicci
de' Medici whom we left in Venice whence we proceeded
with all speed for Augsburg, where the Emperor had assembled 15,000 cavalry. We delivered our message and he
replied in great distress because we had brought no money.
He would now, he told us, be obliged to leave behind the
flower of his army: 5,000 seasoned fighting men who had
no money of their own. For a whole day he held Council,
debating whether to withdraw or press on and finally decided to leave the 5,000 horsemen behind and march by
slow stages with the rest of his forces as far as Trent where
he would await my return with the 50,000 ducats. He gave
me the deed with his seal and signature and asked me to
return to Venice with his treasurer and one of his knights.
I did this, collected the money in Venice and returned with
it to Trent, where I found the Emperor greatly dismayed
over the time lost. Had the money been sent to Augsburg
as he had requested, he would have been in Lombardy
twenty-two days sooner and with the whole of his army.
Moreover, his anxiety turned out to be justified, for the
Duke of Milan turned this respite to good account and
so stiffened his defenses that he was able to inflict loss and
shame both on the Emperor and on our Commune, as I
shall have occasion to relate further on.

On receiving the 50,000 ducats, he distributed them
among his men and immediately started begging and press-
ing me to hasten back for the second installment which he
wanted in Verona. I was reluctant to leave and pointed
out that this journey was unnecessary and would expose me
to a great risk of death and imprisonment. I added that a
more glorious memory would survive me and more honor
reflect on my family if I were to die bearing arms in his
service than if I were to be killed as an agent on my way

[33] Giovanni di Bicci de' Medici was the founder of the great Medici bank.
He was the father of Cosimo, who in 1434 became the most influential figure
in the Florentine state.

to pick up funds. Yet he insisted that I go, saying: "You will serve me better by this journey than you could if you were to command a hundred lances in my service," and added, "Ask me whatever you want and it shall be yours." I said, "Sire, I am happy to go since such is your pleasure, but if I should be killed or captured what sign will my family have to show I died in your service?"

Then he said, "I will give you an emblem from my own coat of arms: the golden lion which you may include among your own armorial bearings. And I ennoble you and your brothers and your descendants." Then he told his chancellor to record this in his register and said to me, "Go and be of good heart, Buonaccorso, for God will be with you in consideration of the deeds I hope to perform as a result of this and, if He grants that I chastise the tyrant of Milan, this emblem I am giving you will be the pledge for great honor and profit which you will one day have from me." He left Trent before I was ready to go and I accompanied him a little way outside the city and left with him Andrea Vettori and Ser Pero da S. Miniato, to whom I entrusted two of my horses and most of my armor except for the breastplate which I preferred to keep on me.

I set out and, on my way through Germany to Venzone, composed one of my doggerel sonnets which I transcribe here:

This current year of fourteen one,
King Rupert, in his town of Trent,
Decreed my scutcheon might henceforth present
An armorial emblem of his own:
The golden lion rampant and, thereon,
Caused to be written in a document
My brothers' names and mine with his assent
So each of us might bear the lion on
His wavy field. Thence our privilege comes,
With lasting patents of nobility,
To bear this symbol bravely on our arms
Wherever such heraldic emblems be
Borne: here or in other realms,

And to hold land from kings in fee.
So, sons and brothers, nobly cultivate
Virtue as befits our new estate.

On the evening of my arrival in Venzone in the Friuli,
I received a visit from a Sienese who kept a spice shop there
with whom I had struck up an acquaintance on my various
journeys through the place. He told me he had got wind of
a plot to capture me on the road the following day. This
was the work of a secret agent of the Duke of Milan: a
Fra Giovanni Dechani who had promised the Lord of Pran-
pergh[34] 4,000 gold ducats if he would deliver me into his
hands, which the said Lord had promised to do on the
pretext of carrying out a reprisal against the Florentines.
I asked the Sienese if I could trust my host and he assured
me that I could. So, about four in the morning I mounted
my horse and, taking the host and a serving boy to guide
me since I would have to go by backroads, made for Porto
Gruaro and did not pause to eat or drink until I got there,
although it was a journey of forty miles. I sent my horses
from there to Padua, and myself set out by sea for Venice.
Later, after the death of the Duke of Milan, I met that
same Fra Giovanni in Bologna, when he confessed that
everything the Sienese had told me was true.

Three days after my arrival in Venice news came that
the Emperor had been defeated outside Brescia and had
withdrawn to Trent, from whence he was prevailed upon
and encouraged by our Commune, the Venetians, and the
Lord of Padua to march to Venzone and thence to Padua.
When he got to Padua, a new delegation arrived from Florence, consisting of Messer Filippo Corsini, Messer Rinaldo
Gianfigliazzi, Messer Maso degli Albizzi, and Messer
Tommaso Sacchetti. They, Andrea Vettori, and myself held
a number of talks and discussions with the Emperor without
managing to reach an agreement. In the end the Emperor
suggested that we all repair to Venice and ask the Venetian
government to mediate and help us reach a compromise.

[34] I have not been able to identify this German nobleman.

We did this, but although we held numerous talks and councils in the presence of the Doge, were so far from achieving a settlement that the Emperor set off for Porto Gruaro in galleys lent him by the Venetians.

When he had gone, the Doge sent for us, expressed great anxiety over this departure, and said: "If you let the Emperor go back to Germany, the Duke of Milan will make himself lord of all Italy." He entreated us to send one or two of our number after him, adding that if we undertook to grant the Emperor the amount he had requested, he too would send a delegation to persuade him to come back to Venice. We agreed to do this and returned to our lodgings. As it turned out that none of the others was eager to undertake this risky journey, I set out alone, with a message from all of us that if he agreed to come back we would give him what he had asked. I caught up with him the following day at a harbor about fifty miles from Venice. On hearing my message, he immediately called a council of his advisers and, as I had told him that a delegation was to come from the Doge too, stayed in his council waiting from sunrise until about the hour of terce, when the legates arrived and were admitted. Shortly afterwards, I too was called in and the Emperor told me that he was willing to return on the understanding that I had pledged my word and that of my colleagues to the effect that, on reaching Venice, he would receive from us the 40,000 ducats which he needed to get his troops in shape. I confirmed this.

He returned to Venice with me and was given the money as promised. From there we went to Padua, where I left him with the rest of our delegation while I returned to Florence to make my report. In due course the other ambassadors also returned, and the Emperor's nephew, Ludwig, Duke of Bavaria, came to initiate further negotiations about aid for the Emperor's journey to Rome and pursuance of the war in Lombardy against the Duke of Milan. The outcome of much talk and parley was our decision against making any further outlay to keep the Emperor in Italy.

This decision would have lost us our liberty had death not overtaken the Duke of Milan so shortly after his capture of Bologna; he died in September after taking the city in June. Had he lived there is no doubt that he would have conquered all of Italy in no time at all, and that we would have fallen under his yoke. For he was already master of Pisa, Siena, Perugia, Chiusi, and all their dependencies; the Malatesta and the Lords of Lucca and Urbino had submitted to him, and all Lombardy except for Venice was under his rule. So it is to his death that we owe our salvation and our power, which is even now on the increase thanks to luck and God's grace and not to the wisdom or virtue of our rulers. For my own impression is that we have grown arrogant and careless. Our leaders are divided amongst themselves and have so sacrified the common good and honor to private grudges and secret feuds that two sorts of citizens, youths and upstarts, have managed, by taking advantage of their dissensions, to worm their way into government. They have grown so overbearing that, were an emperor or great lord to march against us now, our state would certainly collapse. It must surely do so before long unless God restores harmony among our leaders so that they all pull together and stop impeding the course of justice for their own private ends. On this matter I shall write no more for now.

On 28 June 1402, I took up my function as Captain of Barga.[35] On the same day I received news that the army we had sent under Bernardone da Serra to relievé Bologna had been defeated on the way there, at Casalecchio. One result of this defeat was the death of the Lord of Bologna, Giovanni Bentivoglio, on Alberigo Count of Barbiano's taking the city with his army in the name of the Duke of Milan. Of the two Florentine ambassadors who were in the city at the time of its capture, one, Bardo Ritafè, was killed and the other, Niccolò da Uzzano, made prisoner and ransomed some months later. When he returned to Florence he told me that he had been badly tortured and that finally,

[35] Barga is an Apennine town twenty miles north of Lucca.

for fear of further torment, had agreed under duress to write a false confession which he later heard read aloud in Marignano in the presence of the Duke of Milan and his counselors. It concerned the mission with which I had been entrusted when I went to Germany to persuade the new Emperor to come to Italy. In his confession Niccolò declared himself to be responsible for this embassy and stated, along with a number of true things, one which was a complete falsehood. He said that I had been told to use every means at my disposal to deceive the Emperor into believing the Duke of Milan was trying to poison him so as to excite his wrath against the Duke, and that the incident which had ended in the death of the Emperor's physician had been entirely engineered by myself. When the confession had been read, Niccolò confirmed it before the Duke and his council and was led back to prison. He told me all this so that I should beware of falling into the hands of the Duke of Milan and added his apologies and so forth for having exposed me.

Concluding from the above that the Duke of Milan was eager to whitewash himself in the eyes of the Lords of France, I wrote the whole story to the Duke of Orleans, assuring him that it was utterly untrue that I had in any way been the cause of the death of the Emperor's physician, Master Herman, as the Duke of Milan's henchmen were now alleging on the strength of a false confession extracted under torture. I went on to say that, if he advised me to do so, I would be willing to appear before himself, the King and any other Lords he might care to select, in order to defend my honor and prove my innocence in this affair.

While I was Captain of Barga, I received a letter from the Ten on War ordering me to close the roads between Milan and Pisa. Accordingly, I gave instructions for eleven mules to be impounded which had been stopped on the road to Alberguggio from Montecuccoli (which was under the protection of the Duke of Milan) along with their load: twenty-two bales of English wool bought in Pisa by Fran-

cesco Bonconti for Lippo di Muccierello. But no sooner
had the confiscated goods been taken to Barga than the
Lord of Lucca sent a complaint to Florence, claiming that
the wool was the property of Lucchese merchants and de-
manding, with scarcely veiled threats, that it be given back.
Fearing lest he become a declared enemy of our Commune,
our Signoria asked me to hand over the wool to his commissioner, adding that I could leave the mules to whoever
had seized them, since they were the property of subjects
of the Duke of Milan. I did not obey this order but
promptly wrote back, enclosing letters found on one of the
muleteers which confirmed what I have written above, and
begging them to deal fairly with those who had been merely
following orders when they seized the goods. This letter
had little effect, for the Signoria, acting partly from fear
and partly as a result of the pressure of Bartolomeo Corbinelli (a member of the Ten on War, who was, and still is,
a friend of the Lord of Lucca), sent me letters by one of
their marshals ordering me to hand the wool over to him
and threatening me with an exemplary punishment if I
delayed. Having read these letters, I delivered the wool to
the marshal, who gave it into the hands of the Lord of
Lucca's commissioners, after which I distributed the mules
among the men who had impounded them.

Before my term of office at Barga expired, the same
Lord closed the roads between Florence and Lucca, whereupon the Ten on War ordered me to reimpose our blockade
as before. I despatched a notary to tell them that I was
disinclined to disturb the men and soldiers of Barga to
the sole end that their rights be once more overridden at
the petition of the Lord of Lucca. I added that if the Ten
really wished to stop his hostile acts against our Commune,
I was prepared to rouse the whole of upper Garfagnana
against him and had received intelligence that a number of
villages could be wrested from him. If the Commune preferred not to assume overt responsibility for this enterprise,
they could let me proceed by myself. All they need do was
to discreetly convey enough money to me to raise 50 cavalry

and 200 foot-soldiers and archers, and I would declare war
and offer shelter to rebels and deserters from the other
side. Should the Commune wish to dissociate themselves
more completely from my undertaking, I was willing to let
them banish me and imprison my wife and children. They
discussed this proposal and replied that the time was not
ripe for such action, but that they would remember my
offer should the need arise. Later, shortly before the expiry
of my term of office, Master Andrea dell' Ancisa, who was
in Lucca, let me know through a trusted agent of his own
that the Lord of Lucca, having been informed of my plan
by a member of the Ten on War, had arranged for a group
of soldiers belonging to the Duke of Milan to capture me on
my way home to Florence, and had taken precautions to
prevent my taking any but the main road between Barga
and Lucca.

Thanks to this warning, I dallied four days and five
nights in Barga after the expiry of my office. Then, at three
o'clock on 6 January, I set off in the following manner. I
sent my squire before me on horseback, dressed in my
clothes and attended by my servants, while I myself walked,
with a javelin in my hand and a buckler on my arm, surrounded by twenty sturdy foot-soldiers from Barga and
fourteen archers. We reached the bridge at Moriano before
dawn and there I took horse and rode on to S. Gennaro and
from thence to Pescia. We had found the bridge of Ca-
lavorno guarded, but the guards, seeing our strength and
that a number of us were already on the bridge, judged it
prudent to let us pass. The bridge at Chifenti was guarded
too and so heavily that it was impossible for us to get over,
so we made for Moriano where, finding the bridge unguarded, we were able to cross.

During my term in Barga, I received information that a
certain Christofano di Barzuglino was conspiring with men
who had been banished from the town, among whom was a
brother of his own and a man called Nerone. I had Christofano arrested and discovered that this Nerone had put
him up to setting fire to the houses of a great number of

their enemies which, like all the other houses in the town at this time, were full of grain. Since I had come to Barga just at the time Bologna fell to the Duke of Milan, I had taken the precaution of ordering the sheaves to be stacked within the walls. The conspirators counted on the support of all the exiles from Barga and of a number of the Lord of Lucca's foot-soldiers. As soon as they saw the fire, they were to start chopping down one of the gates with the help of some of their own men, who were to have entered through a sewer to set fire to the houses. When I arrested him, his father, Barzuglino, fled. His son had told him all about Nerone's plan and, although the father blamed him roundly for taking part in such a conspiracy, his love for his son prevented his revealing it to me. I sent Christofano to the block, banished his father, and confiscated all his possessions.

On 1 May 1403, I began a term as one of the Standard-bearers of the Militia Companies. My colleagues were Giovanni di Lodovico di Banco, Fantone di Naldo Fantoni, Neri di Ser Frescho, Chello di . . . , a goldsmith, Fruosino di Francesco Spinelli, Lapo di Giovanni Niccolini, Niccolò di Marco Benvenuti, Nofri di Giovanni Siminetti, Antonio di Iacopo del Vingna, Marco di Goro degli Strozzi, Lionardo di Tommaso da Careggi, Vieri di Vieri Guadagni, Bartolomeo di Jacopone Gherardini, Lorenzo di Tommaso Baronci, and Andrea Ciofi, a mason.

That year the Ten on War were informed by a Pisan priest of the existence of an unguarded gate in the city walls of Pisa. This gate had been bricked in years before in such a way that the outer surfaces were flush with the walls while the interior was hollow. The Ten took counsel on this matter with a clever engineer who, having heard them out, went secretly to examine the bricked-in stretch of wall for himself and, seeing the holes left in the exterior by the scaffolding, concluded that it must indeed be hollow. He returned to the Ten and told them that he could poke some gunpowder into these holes, set fire to it and cause an ex-

plosion which would undoubtedly knock down the inner and
outer brick walls.[36]

The Ten appointed two of themselves, Messer Rinaldo
Gianfigliazzi and Messer Filippo Magalotti, and elected
four citizens to go with them: Messer Maso degli Albizzi,
Bartolomeo di Bardo Altoviti, Betto di Giovanni Rustichi,
and myself. We set out for S. Miniato and from thence to
S. Gioconda with all our cavalry and infantry and a large
number of peasants enrolled as foot-soldiers. We left there
Messer Rinaldo, who had fallen ill, and pressed on to seek
lodgings for ourselves and our following at the Abbey of
S. Savino and the houses in its neighborhood. The next day
we stayed there without budging, for news had come that
the Pisans had reinforced the bricked-in door by digging
ditches outside it and had posted a stout guard. We resolved to go to Livorno instead and lay siege to it with all
our equipment and men, but when we got there, found it
manned by a great number of skilled archers. We gave
battle but, after a number of our men had been killed by
crossbow bolts and artillery, gave up and returned to Florence with little honor. I had gone with fourteen horses but
only received pay for four, which came to two gold florins
a day.

On 2 February of that year I became Vicar of Valdinie-
vole, and on 26 April the Signoria sent me as ambassador
to Boucicaut, the governor of Genoa,[37] to protest his confiscation of large quantities of wool and other merchandise
belonging to Florentine merchants. He claimed to be holding this as a guaranty of our good behavior lest we make
war on Messer Gabriello Maria [Visconti], the Lord of
Pisa, who was under the protection of the King of France.

[36] In 1403, Florence was still at war with the Visconti of Milan and with
their Pisan allies.
[37] Marshal Boucicaut became governor of Genoa in 1399, three years after
the city accepted the protection of the French crown. Boucicaut remained in
Genoa until 1409, when Genoese exiles regained control of the city and expelled the French.

He said he had issued a warning before seizing the merchandise, and had only proceeded to seize it after our failure to furnish him with an acceptable reply. The goods were worth 200,000 gold florins and he declared we must accept this loss since our army had attacked Pisa after we had been informed of Messer Gabriello's being received under the King's protection.

My mission from the Signoria was to explain that our forces had not attacked Pisa since hearing of its pact with the King, to sue for the release of our merchants and property, and to promise to make no further moves against Pisa without previously informing Boucicaut. I was able to beg his permission to continue to wage the war which had been started before the Lord of Pisa had sought the King's protection. When I had delivered my message, he told me that he would not return our merchandise until such time as we should have made peace or at least a secure truce with the Lord of Pisa. I wrote this to Florence. The Signoria proceeded to send Messer Filippo Corsini, Messer Rinaldo Gianfigliazzi, Messer Tommaso Sacchetti, and Bartolomeo Corbinelli to Genoa, and charged them and me with the task of convincing Boucicaut that we would commit no further aggressions against the Lord of Pisa. When the four delegates reached Genoa, Boucicaut received us and protracted our talks while he sought to learn whether we had come to make an alliance with him. This was something which he had requested on an earlier occasion, when he had actually reached the stage of discussing terms and conditions with Agnolo di Filippo di Ser Giovanni [Pandolfini], a previous Florentine ambassador. But Agnolo had been obliged to leave the matter in abeyance while he returned to Florence, whence he had promised to return with authority to conclude the pact. He never returned and Boucicaut felt that he had been duped. He confided this to me privately, appealing to me, by my love and loyalty for the King, to tell him whether we had a mandate to sign such an alliance. I swore that as far as I knew we had not, but that I would ask my colleagues. I told them of his inquiry, and they charged me to tell him that they had no such mandate. When I told him their reply, he said: "In that case there was no need of their coming, for I could have reached an understanding more easily and more rapidly with you alone." I went back to the others, and we resolved that Bartolomeo and I should come back to Florence to deliver a report. We did this and, when the Signoria, the Colleges and the Ten on War had heard it, they decided to write to the three ambassadors telling them to sign the truce demanded by Boucicaut for at least three years. They did this and got back the merchandise after going to a great deal more effort than was necessary, if Boucicaut was to be believed, as I have reason to believe he was.

1404. On November 1st I began a term as Prior together with Donato di Michele Velluti, Luigi Mannini, Salvadori di Bondi del Chaccia, Paolo di Cino de' Nobili who was the Standard-bearer of Justice, Simone di Arrigo Bartoli, a needle-vendor, Lapo Martini, Jacopo di Francesco Guasconi, and Giraldo di Lorenzo Giraldi.

On 1 January [1405] I became a Consul of the Wool Guild. My colleagues were: Piero d'Agnolo Capponi, Messer Forese Salviati, Paolo di Piero degli Albizzi, Antonio di Piero di Fronte, Bartolo di Nofri Bischeri, Antonio di Lionardo degli Strozzi, and Sandro di Franco Baroncelli. On the 16th of the same month, I began to serve among the Eight on Security in company with Messer Vanni Castellani, Bertoldo di Messer Filippo Corsini, Guglielmo di Bardo Altoviti, Jacopo di Messer Rinaldo Gianfigliazzi, Agnolo di Giovanni da Pino, Andrea di Berto (a wine seller), and Jacopo di Gilio Schiattesi.

On 15 September, I began to serve among the Twelve Good Men with Niccolò di Niccolò di Gherardini Gianni, Brunetto di Prese da Varazzano, Jacopo Orlandi, Bernardo di Pierozzo Peri, Giovanni di Ser Bernardo Carchelli, Marco di Goro degli Strozzi, Giovanni d'Andrea Minerbetti, Corso Canacci, Agnolo di Filippo di Ser Giovanni [Pandolfini], Piero di Giovanni d'Andrea del Palagio, and Antonio di Giovanni Compagni.

On 5 January [1406], my brother Bartolomeo and I brought our wives to Bagni di Petriolo. Bartolomeo's wife, Lisa, had been ill for a long time and the doctors, being unable to diagnose her illness, had advised her to take the baths. She was cured, returned to Florence and shortly afterwards became pregnant with her first son, for her nine previous children were girls. It therefore seemed to us that those waters had good properties and I note the fact here.

On 17 June 1406, I went as Podesta to Montespertoli, and, during my term of office there, was elected by the Signoria to go as ambassador to King Ladislaus and the Pope in Rome. I refused and was exempted.

On 16 January [1407], I went on an embassy to the Pope[38] in Marseille, and from thence to the King and other Lords in France to try to obtain the release of two of our Commune's ambassadors, Messer Bartolomeo Popoleschi and Bernardo Guadagni, whom the Dukes of Orleans and Burgundy have seized as hostages in reprisal for our having taken Pisa (which they claimed). In Paris, I joined Messer Alberto di Pepo degli Albizzi, my colleague on this mission. In brief, the Duke of Orleans, who was holding the prisoners a three-day ride away at Blois, agreed to let them come to Paris in exchange for our word and theirs that they would not try to leave the city without his permission. They came and it was while their release was being negotiated that the Duke of Burgundy, by an act of foul treachery, had the Duke of Orleans assassinated at three o'clock in the morning of 23 November 1407.[39]

Before the murder, while Messer Alberto and I were at Senlis waiting upon the Duke of Orleans in the hope of prevailing upon him to free the prisoners, the Duke sent for me late one night. He was in a chamber gambling with

[38] The Avignon pope, Benedict XIII.

[39] This murder, which was followed a year later by the assassination of the Duke of Burgundy, intensified the antagonisms between the two rival factions, Armagnac (Orleanist) and Burgundian, competing for control of the French crown.

other lords and when I came in told me he wanted me to play with them. I said that it was more than eight years since I had given up gambling and that, with his permission, I would rather not play, especially since I was an ambassador. But once he had freed the prisoners, I would play with him if he chose to ask me. He said my being an ambassador was a lame excuse, as this should make me all the more eager to please him. I said that I would play so as to please him but that I had only brought enough money from Florence to pay my expenses. At this, he said, "Go on. Sit down and play with my money!" I did and my luck was such that when I rose from the tables I had lost 500 gold scudos. Early next morning, I took horse and rode to Paris to borrow enough money to pay back the Duke and try and make up my losses. The first man from whom I tried to borrow was the ungrateful steward who refused me the 200 florins I asked him. I asked Bartolo di Bernardo di Cino for 100 which he lent me; I borrowed another 100 florins from Luigi di Bartolomeo Giovanni. I then asked Michele de' Pazzi for 300, but he had his money out on loan; so did Baldo di Guido Baldi, from whom I wanted to borrow 400 florins. When I asked Calcidonio degli Alberti for 500 florins, he replied that he didn't have any cash, but that he would give me a bill of exchange for some place. I decided not to make any further demands on my friends, but accepted a bill of exchange from Calcidonio for 500 gold florins, payable in Montpellier.[40] With that sum, and with the loans which I had from Bartolo and from Luigi, I went to see the Duke and handed him a purse containing the 500 gold scudos I owed him. He was delighted and commended my promptness. After dinner, play began and I won back 200 gold scudos. Next day the Duke and all his following moved to Paris. We had many more gambling

---

[40] In effect, Pitti was borrowing money from Calcidonio Alberti, a Florentine banker in Paris, who gave him a bill of exchange payable in Montpellier (in southern France) sometime later and in a different currency. On this type of commercial transaction, see R. de Roover, *The Rise and Decline of the Medici Bank 1397–1494* (Cambridge, Mass., 1963), ch. 6.

sessions up to the time of his death, and in the end I was 2,000 gold scudos to the good.

After his death, Messer Bartolomeo and Bernardo, who had been released from their posts by the Duchess and her sons, returned to Florence. I stayed on in Paris until September, then left for Florence which I reached on 12 October 1407 to find myself a Consul of the Wool Guild.

On 15 December 1408, I began to serve among the officials in charge of the wine tax with Belcaro Serragli, Master Christofano di Giorgio, Michele Acciaiuoli, and Nofri di Palla degli Strozzi.

On 6 July 1409, I took up my post as Captain of Pisa,[41] and the following day Pope Alexander, who had been elected at the Council of Pisa which was then in progress, was crowned. Shortly afterwards, King Louis came to attend the Council as an ally of our Commune. I had played a part in securing this alliance, for I had visited him in Provence on my way back from France, and had had a conversation with him about Florentine politics and about how the Florentines had had a falling out with King Ladislaus. At the end of our talk, he commissioned me to write and tell him when the time seemed ripe for him to enter an alliance with our Commune, adding that unless he heard from me personally he would not send ambassadors. On arriving in Florence, I made a report on all this to the Signoria and the Ten on War, and shortly afterwards, the Ten charged me to write inviting the King to send ambassadors. I did and he complied. After protacted negotiations, the alliance was concluded and the Pope later became a party to it.[42]

---

[41] Pisa had been conquered by Florence in 1406 and was incorporated into the Florentine dominion.

[42] Pope Alexander V was elected pope at Pisa by a group of cardinals from the *curie* of Rome and Avignon. Florence recognized him as the legitimate pope, but none of the major European powers accepted his election as valid. Europe thus had three claimants to the Holy See until 1415, when John XXIII (Alexander's successor) was deposed by the Council of Constance and the Roman pope, Gregory XII, resigned. The Avignon pope, Benedict XIII, refused to resign, but in 1417, the Council elected Oddo Colonna who, as Martin V, was accepted as pope throughout Latin Europe.

While I was Captain of Pisa, I let myself get drawn into a disastrous enterprise. The director of the hospital at Altopascio, Messer Mariano Casassi, was ruining this benefice, had sold many of its possessions, and deserved to be deprived of it. Having ascertained the truth of this, I submitted a petition to Pope Alexander, begging him to take it from Messer Mariano and grant it to my nephew, Cione di Francesco. This I did on the advice of the Cardinal legate of Bologna, Messer Baldassare Cossa—later, by God's grace or disgrace, Pope—who encouraged me with the promise that he would do everything in his power to ensure the success of my venture. Yet, when I had submitted my request and asked him to speak on my behalf to the Pope, he told me, "I cannot keep my promise to you. A certain citizen, against whose will I am loath to go, has dissuaded me from doing so. On the other hand, I will not actively take his part against you either. Get someone to intercede for you, and you will surely be successful." I reproached him and said that I would never have embarked on this enterprise had it not been for his encouragement and promises. But since I had started, I would go through with it in the hope that the justice of my cause would bring me success. Then he confided to me, under the seal of secrecy, that Messer Niccolò da Uzzano was against me and that I should try and win him over. I spoke to Niccolò in Messer Bartolomeo Popoleschi's presence, telling him what I had heard. He replied that, being deeply obliged to Messer Mariano, he had not refused to speak on his behalf. Moreover, he had been unaware of my interest in the matter but now that he knew of it he would refrain from speaking for either party. He gave me his word to this effect in the presence of Messer Bartolomeo. The way he kept it was to immediately incite all his friends and henchmen, in particular Bartolomeo di Niccolò Valori and Gino di Neri Capponi, to maneuver openly against me.

However, I did not withdraw from this unfortunate undertaking, partly because, at this point, it seemed impossible to do so with honor, partly because I still hoped for justice and Messer Mariano's dismissal. So, despite the

great cost, I persisted in my suit. As soon as my term of
office was ended, I went to Bologna to see the Pope and
passed two months there to no avail except that I spent a
lot of money. Then I came back to Florence, went for another month to Bologna and came back again to Florence.
Meanwhile Pope Alexander died and Pope John[43] was
elected. I went to see him and stayed a month, at the end
of which he had Luigi da Prato tell me that if I made peace
with Messer Niccolò da Uzzano he would make sure that
I was satisfied. He told the same thing to Bartolomeo
Popoleschi who was there on an embassy with Niccolò. I
told them both that I was ready to do as the Pope wished.
Messer Bartolomeo approached Niccolò who declared himself willing to make peace with myself and my brothers in
Florence and be friends with us. I went back to Florence
and, when the other two had returned, Messer Bartolomeo
arranged a meeting between my brothers and myself and
Niccolò in S. Piero Scheraggio. After a great deal of con-
ciliatory talk, Niccolò promised to do nothing more against
us. The way he kept this promise was to get Mariano
Casassi to receive a son of Giovanni di Lodovico di Banco
as a monk in Altopascio, and to make the hospice over to
him with all its possessions under the jurisdiction of the
Florentine Commune, while he himself retired to Lucca.

On 24 July 1410, I went to Rome as a commissioner for
our Commune with Messer Jacopo Salviati and King Louis
of France to make war on King Ladislaus. We stopped off
on the way at Montepulciano where we spent 24 days trying to engage Sforza da Cutignola to fight for us at our expense. We finally managed to do so but with difficulty as he
had already signed a pact with King Ladislaus. When we
had finally won him over, we paid him 25,000 florins and
pressed on to Rome. When we had been there a month
Messer Jacopo returned to Florence to report on some
urgent matters and I stayed on in Rome. The King was lin-
gering there unable to take the field, for he had been failed

[43] Pope John XXIII, elected in 1410, and deposed by the Council of Constance in 1415.

by the three leading captains, Paolo Orsini, Sforza da Cutignola, and Braccio da Montone, and by the Pope, who had reneged on his promise to send the money which was to have been paid to Paolo Orsini. So, on the last day of December, the King left Rome for Florence. On our way north we received letters describing the peace treaty which our commune had concluded with King Ladislaus. The French King was highly incensed at the news and said, "They might at least have waited until our alliance had expired; yet it lasts the whole month of January!" We parted at Prato, whence he set out for Bologna and I for Florence. After spending a week there, I went to Bologna at my own expense to look after the Altopascio lawsuit. When I had been there about twenty days, and after several audiences with the Pope, entreating him to look kindly on my case, he told me that he could not see his way towards granting my request on account of certain promises he had made which he did not want to break. He added that he was ready to make it up to me in any other way he could, and would I be interested in a good bishopric? I reproached him bitterly, saying I wanted nothing else from him and came away greatly dissatisfied. I complained about the matter to King Louis, took my leave of him and returned to Florence.

The following March the Pope and King Louis went to Rome. I went to Prato to see the king on his way through, and he insisted on my coming with him as far as Siena. He wanted me to go with him to Rome and offered me money, horses, and a salary. I decided against going, thinking that if I did the Signoria might well order me back lest it seem that I had gone as a representative of our Commune. I therefore took leave of him and returned to Florence where I stayed until 25 April 1411, when I took my family to Pisa to escape the plague which had broken out in Florence. I took with me Nerozzo and Doffo di Luigi and Giovanozzo di Francesco, my first cousins, as well as two servants, a serving boy and a wet nurse for a fifteen-month old baby.

In Pisa I rented a furnished house from Bindo and Jacopo and Filippo degl' Astai for 48 gold florins. Towards the end of June, one of the servants died of the pestilence, and a fortnight later my twelve-year-old daughter also died. After that, I decided to leave that house and went to stay outside Pisa in a place belonging to Tommaso Grassolini, who rented it to me for twenty florins until 24 November when we came back to Florence. I reckoned that I had spent 1,300 florins in seven months. The place where we stayed is called Ghezano.

. . .

That you, our sons and descendants, and whoever else may chance to read or hear read what I have written here, may learn what happens when one tries, no matter how rightfully, to resist those mightier than oneself.

In 1404, when my brother Luigi was Podestà of Bucine and Valdambra, the Abbot of S. Piero a Ruota in Valdambra[44] submitted a number of reasonable requests to him which Luigi settled with promptitude and courtesy. After this, the Abbot grew very fond of Luigi as he had occasion to show three years later when he sought refuge in our house—where he had already stayed several times, for we had come to regard him as our spiritual father—from certain great and mighty personages who had taken advantage of his age to molest him. He told us that the abbacy, which he had held for thirty-four years, had become too much for him now that he was old and infirm, and that he had decided to give it up. He wanted us to act as his procurators, renounce the benefice in his name and, at the same time, try to obtain it for one of our own sons. We tried to dissuade him from his resolve, promising that if he remained on in his abbey, we would give him all our help and support. Yet in the end, after a great deal of discussion, we agreed to act for him, although we were resolved in our own minds to keep him in his abbacy and furnish him all the aid he might

[44] The Valdambra is a district west of Arezzo; its stream joins the Arno near Montevarchi.

need to maintain it. He went back to the abbey and, shortly afterwards, Albertaccio Ricasoli and his henchmen contrived to implicate him in a sham conspiracy and then to denounce him to the Ten on War for plotting to hand over Valdambra to the Ubertini, who were in rebellion against the Commune. The Ten ordered the Abbot's arrest, but his suspicions had already been aroused by the visit of a bogus manservant who, choosing a moment when he was absent, had called at the abbey and told the local men who saw him that he had come with a message for the Abbot from Andreino degl' Ubertini and was awaiting a reply. After the man's departure, the Abbot returned and, on learning what had been said, galloped at full speed to our house and told us the whole story. Luigi took him to see the Ten, who carefully examined him and, having established the falsity of their informer, let him go back to his monastery.

Knowing the might and obstinacy of the Ricasoli, I concluded from this that they would not rest until by force or trickery they had got their hands on the abbey—unless we hastened to submit the Abbot's renunciation and our own petition. The rest of the family disagreed with me, fearing that we would be criticized, especially since the Abbot, comforted by the aid we had extended to him on several occasions since becoming his procurators, had greatly recovered his spirits. I spoke to him and made Luigi speak to him about the risks he was running in maintaining the abbacy, and he replied that he would accept whatever decision we might reach but begged us to have a care for his honor. Francesco and Luigi took this to mean he did not want us to proceed with the renunciation, but Bartolomeo and I thought it better to do so in the interests of his own safety.

The Ricasoli saw that we had come out openly on the side of the Abbot and that they could not achieve their ends by tricking the Commune into helping them. So they had four of their number (Pandolfo, Bindaccio, Galeotto, and Carlo) who were in Rome draw up a number of false charges against the Abbot and formally denounce him to

Pope John (whose equerries and chamberlains they were). The Abbot was summoned to appear and answer these charges but, being old, unfit to travel, and, moreover, fearful that if he went to Rome he might suffer some harm to his person at the hands of his powerful enemies, resolved to send Ser Giuliano dalla Cicogna, a friend of mine who was a priest at S. Lorenzo, to act as his legal representative.

Then Luigi and I interceded with Albertaccio, begging him tactfully to abandon the case against the Abbot for our sake, and explaining how very close we were to the Abbot and how we had hoped to have the abbey for one of our sons. He replied that he had not known of our arrangement, that if he had he would not have denounced the Abbot even though he was an enemy. He said that he could not now withdraw from the undertaking without the agreement of his relatives in Rome, but that he would write to them.

Having heard that Ridolfo di Bonifazio Peruzzi, a relative of Albertaccio's, was in league with him to request the abbacy for his brother, Arnoldo, we went to see him, told him of our connection with the Abbot, and begged him to withdraw from the affair for our sake. He said he had not meddled with it and would not do so. We then went to see Messer Rinaldo Gianfigliazzi, Albertaccio's father-in-law, told him the whole story and begged him to persuade Albertaccio to give up the case. He promised to do his best.

Next, we went to the Priors' Palace and appealed to the Signoria and Colleges to write a letter to the Pope, requesting that he instruct the Bishop of Florence or Arezzo or Fiesole, or any other local prelate, to investigate the charges made against the Abbot and, on their findings, judge himself of the Abbot's guilt or innocence. When we had submitted our petition, Betto Busini, a member of one of the Colleges who had been put up to this by the Peruzzi, asked the Signoria to give our opponents a hearing. The Signoria told us we must come back again, as they wanted both parties in the dispute to be present. We returned next day and, when the Colleges had assembled, in came Michele di Messer Vanni Castellani, Papino di Messer Rinaldo [Gian-

figliazzi], Piero di Giovanni di Piero Baroncelli, and Ridolfo Peruzzi's brother, Bindaccio. They all spoke before
the Colleges, begging them to refuse the letter I had requested. I was called to speak for our side. I went in and
Bindaccio Peruzzi followed me. I asked that the letter be
sent. Bindaccio, whose family were trying to obtain the abbacy for his brother, spoke against my request and vilified
the Abbot. We withdrew, and the outcome was that the
Ricasoli faction had their way and the letter was not written.

Meanwhile in Rome, the case against the Abbot had been
entrusted to Cardinal Orsini, who refused to accept the ap-
pearance of a representative in lieu of the Abbot himself.
Ser Giuliano handed him a letter from me, for I had tried
when in Pisa to enlist this Cardinal as our patron and had
presented him with a goblet of gilded silver which had cost
me 32 florins. On presenting the letter, Ser Giuliano said,
"Your Eminence, I beseech you to look with favor on the
Abbot for the sake of Buonaccorso who is your devoted
servant and that of our Holy Father." At this Pandolfo
Ricasoli, who was present and had overheard, broke in,
crying, "Your Eminence, he has just named a thorough
enemy of Holy Church and Our Lord the Pope! Buonaccorso's brother, Luigi, was the ringleader and chief partisan
among the Priors of the peace signed by the Commune of
Florence with King Ladislaus in defiance of Holy Church
and of Our Lord the Pope!" After that the Ricasoli, who
were constantly around the Pope, kept bringing up the matter of Luigi and the peace, which was undeniable and
greatly displeasing to him, and so thoroughly turned him
against us that ever since we have suffered open and secret
persecution at his hands and at those of his clique in this
city, chief of whom are Messer Rinaldo Gianfigliazzi, Gino
Capponi, Bartolomeo Valori, Niccolò da Uzzano, and their
henchmen and satellites.

The outcome of the case against the Abbot was that the
Pope, with a gross and flagrant disregard for justice, deprived him of his benefice, condemned him to perpetual im-

prisonment and granted the abbey to Arnoldo Peruzzi. When Bindaccio and his brother had obtained the papal licence, they petitioned our Signoria to grant them possession. A committee of three jurists was formed to study the matter.

While the litigation was in progress, I asked the Signoria for a guard to ensure the Abbot's safety and had him come to Florence to defend his cause. By the time he, a monk, Ser Giuliano, and the latter's brother, Francesco, had been a month in my house, it had become clear that he would lose his case, both on account of the papal bulls excommunicating him and any who helped or favored him, and of the power of his opponents, who had produced numerous false witnesses to back up their calumnies against him and us. One day I was deploring our situation with Ser Giuliano, saying that I saw no hope in persisting when the sides were so unevenly matched. We had against us the power of the Gianfigliazzi, the Castellani, the Peruzzi, and all the other friends, relatives, henchmen, and followers of the Ricasoli. Then he said to me, "I see a way. Let the Abbot submit a petition to the Signoria denouncing Albertaccio [Ricasoli]. If he does this, Albertaccio will run the risk of being declared a magnate and will be forced to come to some sort of compromise with him." [45] I told him the idea appealed to me and that he should work it out with the Abbot, but that I did not wish to be involved. Then he said, "Tell your servant, Santi, to do what I tell him and leave the rest to me."

At one o'clock the next morning Ser Giuliano said to the Abbot, "Let us go and visit Messer Giovanni di Ser Ristoro to beg for his help with your case." Then he told his brother to take Santi and Messer Lapo Ricasoli, an old enemy of Albertaccio's side of the family who happened to be dining with us that night, to hide near Messer Gi-

---

[45] For certain crimes against citizens which were not prosecuted in the regular courts, individuals could be denounced to the Signoria. By a two-thirds vote of the Priors and the Colleges, such individuals could be declared magnates, and thus ineligible for the major offices of the Commune.

ovanni's house. When the Abbot and his monk passed by on their way back here, they were to fall on them, assault them—without however harming them—and flee. They did this and, as neither the Abbot, the monk, nor the guard from the Signoria knew what was afoot, they firmly believed that either Albertaccio or some other had intended to thrash or injure the Abbot but had taken to his heels at the sight of the Signoria's guard. They went straight to the Priors' Palace and lodged a complaint with the Signoria. That very night, the Priors issued a proclamation to the effect that anyone who knew the culprit and failed to reveal his name within three days would be liable to penalties against their persons and property, but that the culprit would be freely absolved if he gave himself up. The following day, in session with the Colleges, the Signoria made this an official decree.

The assailants returned to our house and were shortly followed by the Abbot, so that I heard the story twice: first from the aggressors who told me the truth, and then from the Abbot and his companions who added some lies, pretending they had been struck and mauled, and claiming to have recognized Carlo Ricasoli who was back from Rome. The next day, Carlo was summoned before the Podestà and, knowing himself to be innocent, obeyed the summons. He was imprisoned in the chapel. On the evening of the same day, Giuliano was arrested by the guards of the Podestà at the instigation of Albertaccio and Papino di Messer Rinaldo [Gianfigliazzi], who suspected that he might know something of the affair. The Podestà merely interrogated him however and then let him go, saying, "Come back tomorrow morning." He came back here and told me of his arrest, and when I heard this and of the decree which had been promulgated, I had him and Messer Lapo and Santi and Francesco leave the house. I also sent Brando da Chachiano di Chianti to Val di Pesa, for although he had taken no part in the unfortunate business, he had known about it. Next day, the Podestà first summoned Ser Giuliano and later myself. I obeyed the summons. He told me that unless I produced Ser Giuliano he would take action against me. I said I did not know where he was. He let me go but sent for me again the next day and was of a mind, as I heard later, to lock me up. I presented myself and he questioned me and threatened me and finally let me go on the understanding that I was to return next day. After that, I made up my mind to go before the Signoria on the morrow and tell them all I knew. I was afraid that if I didn't someone else might, and the new decree would be invoked against me. So I did this and, when they had heard my story, the Signoria sent a note instructing the Podestà to start proceedings against those whose names I had given: my manservant Santi, Francesco dalla Cicogna, the brother of the priest Giuliano, and any further accomplices he might discover. They were all to suffer banishment and confiscation of their property while I, if any guilt attached to me, was to be granted a free pardon. The Podestà proceeded to accuse Santi, the priest Giuliano and his brother, Messer Lapo Ricasoli, Brando da Chachiano di Chianti, and myself. We were all summoned, but the others feared torture and did not present themselves. I was interrogated and released on paying a surety of 3,000 florins. When the time limits set by the Podestà had elapsed, he sentenced Santi to pay 800 florins, Messer Lapo, Francesco, the priest, and Brando to 500 florins each and to banishment from Florence and its territory for three years. I was pardoned.[46]

And mark that, during the trial, Messer Michele Castellani, Papino Gianfigliazzi, and the others I named earlier did everything in their power, both in public and in private, to have me banned from office. The whole clique of underhand plotters worked tirelessly against me too, and chief among these was Niccolò Barbadori, whose cabals and machinations were reported to my by the Podestà himself and by the judge adjutant, Messer Tommaso. Many friends

[46] Pitti's description of these events tallies closely with the account of the case in the records of the criminal courts; *ASF, Atti del Podestà*, 4272, no pagination, 17 December 1412.

and relatives spoke up for me, particularly Giovanni Carducci, Migliore di Giunta Migliore, Rinaldo di Messer Maso [degli Albizzi], Piero di Luca degli Albizzi, Messer Cristofano degli Spini, Messer Francesco Machiavelli, Nofri Bischeri, Sandro di Vieri Altoviti, Currado Panciatichi, Guidetto Guidetti, Francesco Canigiani, and many other citizens, including my trusty friend Roberto de' Rossi, whose help was invaluable and who managed to win the judge adjutant over to my side.

The Signoria demanded a heavy sentence because of the slight to their guard who had been with the Abbot. Messer Lapo and Santi, my manservant, paid their fines and went into exile. The other four were declared outlaws. I have recorded this unfortunate affair and named those who did me disservice and the principal friends who rallied to me, not so that you, my sons and descendants, may seek to be revenged on those who harmed us, but rather so that you may show gratitude towards the descendants of our friends. And, as I said at the beginning of this entry, take example from this case wherein we suffered from trying to vie with the powerful, meddling in squabbles over Church benefices and getting involved with priests. Have no dealings with them and you will be wise.

On 16 May 1413, I began a term among the Eight on Security at the same time as Simone Salviati, Marco di Goro degli Strozzi, and Giovanni di Bicci de' Medici. Four colleagues were already in office: Riccardo di Niccolò di Mone, Giovanni di Francesco Caccini, Brando della Badessa, and Piero di Giovanni del Palagio, who finished their term on 1 June and were replaced by Astorre di Niccolò di Gherardino Gianni, Antonio di Vanni Manucci, Guccio da Sommaia, and Banco di Sandro.

At two o'clock in the morning of 24 June, the Eve of St. James's Day of that same year—a disastrous one for myself and my brothers—the Executor and Captain sent one of his officers to arrest me. When I presented myself, he had me locked in a chamber. At dawn they brought in my brother, Bartolomeo, whom they had arrested in Val di Pesa, and put him in another room. At about nine o'clock the Executor informed us that we would be held until our brother, Luigi, obeyed his summons and appeared before him. Luigi was accused of having revealed some secret deliberations in the Priors' Palace to the ambassadors of King Ladislaus. This had been discovered when a letter from these Ambassadors to the King fell into the hands of the Ten. Officials of the Executor had gone to Luigi's house to arrest him only to find he had left several days earlier for Naples, or, more precisely, for Aquila. The Executor instructed me to write Luigi that if he failed to return and face the charges against him, Bartolomeo and myself would be made to suffer for it. I wrote and despatched my own courier with my letter and the official summons.

My friends and relatives assembled about 200 prominent citizens in S. Piero Scheraggio where my nephew, Neri di Piero, addressed them and begged for their support and counsel. From there, they proceeded in a body to implore the Signoria for our release and, later the same morning, called on the Executor and strongly exhorted him in the same vein. Messer Rinaldo Gianfigliazzi delivered the address to the Executor and Messer Filippo Corsini spoke before the Signoria. Again, on the 31st of the month, all our womenfolk and children who were in Florence went to the Palace when the Signoria and the Colleges and the Ten were in session and implored our release. Deciding that we had in fact been wrongly used, they gave orders for our release and, sending for the Executor, instructed him to carry them out, which he did.

The sequel was that when Luigi got my letter and the writ of summons in Naples, he begged King Ladislaus's permission to depart and set off at once, only to hear on reaching Perugia that he had been banished.[47] And so he had, for his name had been publicly called with the sound of trumpets, and he had been allowed three days to obey the

---

[47] Luigi's condemnation is in *ASF, Atti del Esecutore degli Ordinamenti della Giustizia*, 1808, fols. 68r–69r. The sentence was cancelled on 20 October 1414.

summons. When these elapsed, he was condemned to perpetual banishment and loss of property, and all our efforts
to have a term set to his banishment were of no avail. He
returned to Aquila where, with our brother Francesco as
his lieutenant, he had already served one year as Captain
and had been reappointed by the King to serve another.
Leaving Francesco there, he went to Naples where he renounced the office, for war was about to break out between
our Commune and the King as a result of the ruthless machinations of the papal faction within our city. When he had
renounced the office, he received a letter from the King
telling him that the review usually held on an outgoing of-
ficeholder's administrative term would be waived in his
case and in that of any officials he had brought to Aquila.
Before these letters reached Aquila, Francesco had died.
May his soul rest in peace. We held his funeral here on 9
October of that accursed year.

I said "accursed year," but in fact we have had almost
four disastrous years, for our opponents keep harrying and
hounding us and never miss a chance to humiliate us or do
us an ill turn. This is in revenge for the part Luigi played,
when he was a prior in December 1410, in promoting the
peace treaty with King Ladislaus. That faction always re-
sented the peace and in their eagerness to please the Pope,
who has suborned them with gifts of benefices and the
promise of more, have so cunningly contrived to undermine
it that today—30 October 1413—they seem very close to
achieving their ends. They have persuaded the citizenry
that the King's capture of Rome and other papal possessions portends his doing the same with our own territory
and liberty, and have generally aroused a mood of suspicion
and unrest. I myself am not sure that the King may not
have conceived such a design, but if he has the fault lies
with the provocative and bellicose behavior in which the
papal clique in Florence have indulged ever since peace was
signed against the Pope's will. For a year after our Commune's withdrawal from the field, King Louis and the
Pope continued the war against King Ladislaus. It was not

until 1412, when King Louis had returned to France and King Ladislaus was marching on Rome with a great army, that the Pope lost heart and made peace with him. As soon as he had made it, he set about trying to persuade the Emperor to come to Italy. Suspecting this move to be directed against himself, King Ladislaus sent urgent protests to our Signoria and a number of embassies requesting us to enter a defensive alliance with himself or, alternatively, to guarantee that the Pope would not bring the Emperor from Germany to make war on him. Both the alliance and the guarantee were refused. On being thus denied, King Ladislaus marched with a great army on Rome, captured it and would have captured the Pope and his cardinals too, but they fled to Florence. Since coming here, the Pope has been maneuvering to get us to form a league with him to make war on the King. By distributing benefices and promises of benefices, he has won over so many influential citizens that I think he will succeed in his design and, though I pray God that our Commune may avoid war, I have little hope of it. The expense of such a war would be crippling and would place us in dire straits. So may God prevent it in such a way that we retain our freedom.

On 8 June 1413, Pope John fled from Rome, which had been captured by King Ladislaus, and paused at S. Antonio del Vescovo, whither the Priors went to meet and pay their respects to him. He stayed there until the . . . of November, while his courtiers and cardinals found lodgings in Florence, and, while there, he drew up and signed the act of alliance with this Commune. Then he went on to Bologna.

In November of that year, the Captains of the Parte Guelfa[48] took counsel with a large number of Guelfs who

[48] The Parte Guelfa was established in the thirteenth century as the political organization of the Florentine Guelfs, in its struggle with the Ghibellines. With the triumph of Guelfism, the Parte became a powerful and influential branch of the communal government. However, its authority declined in the later decades of the fourteenth century; by 1412, it no longer played a significant role in Florentine politics. Nor did the reforms described by Pitti rejuvenate this moribund society.

had been assembled, and also with the two regular councils of One Hundred and of Sixty. With their colleges and with ninety-six Guelf coadjutors, they assumed the authority for reforming offices of the Parte with a new scrutiny, after burning and annulling all of the previous scrutinies. They were motivated to do this, because the Parte had lost much of its accustomed honor and reputation. So low indeed had it fallen that the Captains had difficulty in recruiting citizens to accompany them on their processions to make the customary offerings. This resulted from the disdain felt by good and true Guelfs at seeing many Ghibellines and parvenus of low condition occupying the offices of the Parte Guelfa.

That year [1413], my name was drawn as Podestà for Pieve a S. Stefano. At first I thought it would be best to go in order to put some distance between myself and the opponents who had sought my death. But on second thought it seemed better to refuse, for my adversaries seemed to be weakening now that the citizens, realizing they were trying to lead us to war in order to please the Pope, had begun to turn against them. Accordingly, I resolved to refuse the office, and submitted a petition to this effect to the Signoria and Colleges, who granted it with a large majority. The papal faction heard of this and, calculating that if I remained in Florence I would necessarily be drawn as Standard-bearer of Justice at the beginning of July, contrived that Barduccio Cherichini, who was Standard-bearer of Justice at that time, should delay calling the Council of the Popolo until a new College of Twelve should have been elected, which was due to happen in a fortnight. I resubmitted my petition to the newly formed Twelve but, though it was put to the vote repeatedly, it did not pass, being blocked by the cabals of the papal faction. So in the end, I was denied [my petition], and had perforce to go and serve as Podestà, which I did with great reluctance and at the expense of my health.

When I got back to Florence in mid-June, 1414, Maso degli Albizzi was Standard-bearer of Justice. At the end of that month, peace was signed with King Ladislaus despite the vigorous opposition of the papal faction. The King, who claimed that our brother Luigi had been wrongfully banished, wanted his recall to be stipulated in the peace treaty. But when I heard this from Luigi's brother-in-law, Gabriello Brunelleschi, the King's ambassador, I firmly opposed it and did everything I could to prevent such a condition being inserted. Since Luigi was innocent, I did not want his recall to come about as a concession to the King. I had great trouble convincing Gabriello and a group of our friends and relatives who had heard of the King's proposal and welcomed it, as they feared we would not otherwise succeed in having the banishment revoked.

That September, when Messer Vanni Castellani was Standard-bearer of Justice, we petitioned the Signoria and the Colleges for an amnesty for Luigi and received it. After his return we requested that his banishment be rescinded and obtained this too, despite the obstacles put in our way by the usual cabal. He was officially recalled and restored to full civic rights that same year.

That year I left Florence on 5 October for Pisa, where I boarded one of three galleys which had come from Provence to bring Pope John to Avignon. I disembarked at Fréjus where I bought three packhorses to which I added a fourth at Avignon. At Tarascon I visited King Louis, who welcomed me warmly. On leaving him, I went to Paris by way of the Alps and Auvergne. In Paris, I tried to collect the balance of what the Count of Savoy owed me and to claim the estate of Luigi di Bartolomeo Giovanni who had named my nephews, Neri and Giovanni, as his heirs. Letters came to me from Florence with the news that my name had been drawn as Vicar of the Upper Valdarno. On learning this, I left Paris (on 12 January) and went to Avignon and from there to Arles to call on King Louis, and then through Provence to Marseille where I planned to board one of the galleys he was having readied to send to Naples. On finding that these were not due to leave for another fortnight, and fearing to arrive too late to take up office on 1 March, I resolved to go overland via Nice and Genoa. When I was two leagues from Nice, I sent ahead to ask for a safe-conduct pass but was refused. I went to a village called Cagne which belongs to Giorgino and Onorato de' Grimaldi. They were delighted to see me and gave me a great welcome. I asked them to help me fit out a brig at Antibes so that I could bypass Nice for Monaco or Menton, and begged them to get my horses through Nice by passing them off as their own. They willingly agreed to do this but, just as we had made up our minds, a relative of theirs arrived from Nice who, hearing of our plan, warned us that there was a small galley lying in the river mouth at Nice, for what purpose nobody knew. This aroused my suspicions, especially as I had heard that the whole Riviera was in a state of unrest and that travellers were being robbed and murdered. I decided to go back to Marseille and await the departure of the galleys which left finally on 14 February, and I with them aboard a small galley. We were so delayed by gales that it took us seventeen days to reach Porto Pisano. The small galley was separated from the others and at one point it looked as though we were going to be blown towards the Barbary Coast. Yet, by the grace of God, we reached Porto Pisano on 2 March after a most wearisome and harrowing passage. We were cooped up in that small craft listening to the captain groaning and crying, "We are being blown towards Barbary! They'll take us and sell us as slaves!" And all the time I worried that our enemies would prevent my brothers from deferring the start of my term in office, so that I would arrive late and thus be banned from office for two years. When I reached Pisa, I heard from Filippo del Toccio that I had been granted leave until the end of March. I came back to Florence and was at my post on 6 March, and, by God's grace, spent a useful and enjoyable term in that office and returned thence with honor.

. . .

On 26 October 1417, my name was drawn as Standard-
bearer of Justice from the purses set up in 1391 but, as I
was found to be listed in the book of tax delinquents for
having failed to pay three forced loans levied on citizens
who left the city to avoid the pestilence, I was declared
ineligible. This was unfair for, according to the law, the
deadline for paying these loans had not yet elapsed. But
the Signoria and Colleges had shortened the time limit and
published this decision in Florence so that I, who was in
Pisa, did not hear of it and suffered thereby.

.   .   .

In 1419, Antonio di Giovanni di Messer Zanobi da Mezzola was arrested in Siena and condemned to be hanged.
He had been declared an outlaw on account of a woman
from there with whom he had run off. His relatives implored our Signoria's ambassador to intercede on his behalf
with the Commune and Signoria of Siena and beg for his
release. This was granted and the ambassador brought
Antonio back with him to Florence.

Meanwhile I, who was Podestà at Montepulciano, im-
posed a fine of 600 florins on Andrea di Salimbene degli
Scotti of Siena, an inhabitant of Montepulciano, for having
traded in grain against the orders and statutes of that
Commune. In accordance with the statute, I gave him
twenty days to pay and let him out on bail. He went to
Siena and prevailed on the Sienese ambassador to go to
Florence and petition our Signoria to cancel the sentence.
When the Commune of Montepulciano heard this, they sent
two ambassadors of their own to beg the Florentine Signoria and Colleges to respect their statutes. Both sides were
given a hearing. The matter was put to the vote, and the
decision was that the Priors and Council of Montepulciano
might take whatever course they thought fit. The reason
for this was that the Commune of Montepulciano has not
the right to remit fines of more than 500 Cortona *lire*
(worth 400 *lire* in Florentine currency), that the money
from all fines belongs to the Commune of Montepulciano,

and that the Signoria may not decide matters relating to Montepulciano unless it is in plenary session with the Colleges. The ambassadors from Montepulciano attacked this decision, for they were distrustful of what their own government might do. The question was put to the vote forty-six times in two days. Finally, on the insistence of the Standard-bearer of Justice, Giovanni Minerbetti, and of Piero di Fronte and Giovanni Luigi Mannini, who, at the behest of the Ricasoli—still animated by their old grudge against myself—had come out strongly for Andrea, the case was decided in his favor. The Signoria wrote to the Commune of Montepulciano ordering the sentence against him be annulled. They sent me a stiff note, bidding me carry out their instructions and remit all Andrea's expenses, including fees due to myself and the prosecutor, the cancellation tax and any others which might arise.

I summoned the Council who, on hearing this letter and my own, resolved to send another two ambassadors to the Signoria and Colleges. They asked that, if Andrea's fine was to be remitted, he should at least be forced to pay the two *soldi* in the *lira* called for by the statutes. For if he did not, they could not cancel his debt without grave prejudice to themselves, and the cancellation would not be valid if they did. The ambassadors were told not to submit their petition to the Signoria unless the Colleges were present.

In the meantime, Andrea had returned to Siena and got the ambassador to go to Florence with him once more. Both parties to the dispute were waiting in the courtroom for the Signoria and Colleges to assemble, when Pandolfo Ricasoli, knowing the envoys from Montepulciano wanted to speak to the Signoria in the presence of the Colleges, sent a relative of his, a member of one of the Colleges, to inform the Signoria, who immediately called them in. The envoys explained that their instructions were to speak before those to whom their letter of credence was addressed. They were asked to hand the letter over and state their business right away. They had no choice but to state it. The answer given them was that they should return at once to

Montepulciano with the message that the Signoria desired to be obeyed. The Signoria then wrote me a letter reiterating their demands. I also received letters from my son and Filippo Machiavelli, which warned me that if I did not hasten to obey I would be courting ruin and humiliation. So I resolved to override my own impulse, which was to resist the unjust order at the cost, if need be, of banishment. I summoned the Council and persuaded them to declare all Andrea's debts to myself and others completely remitted. Fearing lest the irregularity of this Council decision might cause him trouble in the future, Andrea went to Florence and came back with a letter to me from the Signoria which I shall copy out here.

> Priors of the Guilds and Standard-Bearer of Justice of the Popolo and Commune of Florence.
> In two earlier letters, we asked you to ensure that the sentence passed by you on Andrea Lancianti be completely annulled and cancelled, and that no payment be exacted from him for any reason whatsoever. We had supposed you to be a good citizen imbued with proper reverence for this Signoria. Had you been so, our order would have been obeyed and we would not be forced to write to you again on this matter. We now find that the sentence against Andrea has not been cancelled, since certain citizens have been authorized to make rulings with regard to it. This astonishes us. Yet the aim and method of such dilatoriness has not escaped us, and we are greatly incensed at your disobedience. Wherefore, we charge and enjoin you to ensure, on receipt of this letter, that the qualified officials declare Andrea exempt from the said fine, that all claims against him (on the part of the Commune, the prosecutor, yourself and any others) be declared null and void, and that no debts arising from this case be exacted from him. We urge you to see to this without delay, for we are determined to be obeyed. Lest you have any doubts about this, we have sentenced you to pay 1,000 gold florins to the treasury of the Commune if, by the 15th of this current April, Andrea and his guarantors have not been exempted and released, according to the usages of local law, from the aforementioned fine as previously demanded. If you have complied with our order by that date, the sentence brought against you will be annulled at the discretion of

the Signoria. Furthermore, should you have failed by then to do our bidding, we desire your judge, police official, and notaries to appear before this Signoria on the 16th of this current April. We shall accept the bearer's word that he has given this into your hands. Florence, 16 April 1420.

On the top was written: to Buonaccorso the son of Neri dei Pitti, Podestà of Montepulciano, gentleman and citizen of Florence.

On receiving this letter, I convoked the Council of Fifty and the General Council and had them annul Andrea's sentence. He wrote to tell the Signoria in Florence that he was satisfied. I too wrote an account of what had been done, and so did the Priors. On the basis of all these letters, the Signoria declared the sentence against me annulled, and my son, Luca, paid the cancellation tax to the Florentine treasury. So ends my account of the wrong the Signoria, spurred thereto by the Ricasoli clique, did me on the pretext of repaying the Sienese for their clemency towards that man from the Mezzola family.

. . .

On 1 July 1422, I became Standard-bearer of Justice. The Priors who served with me were Buonaccorso di Paolo Corsellini, a brazier, Baldo di Nofri di Baldo, a belt-maker, Bernardo di Bartolomeo Gherardi, Simone di Lapo di Francesco Corsi, Domenico di Bartolo Ottavanti, Manno di Giovanni di Temperano Manni, Paolo di Berto Carnesecchi, Antonio di Tommaso di Guccio Martini.

. . .

While I was Standard-bearer, we sent an ambassador to Rome. We received Messer Tommaso da Campo Fregoso, the Lord of Sarzana, under our protection. We enlisted Braccio da Montone, the Lord of Perugia, with 1,000 lances and 300 footsoldiers. We entered a five-year alliance with the Lord of Lucca, sent ambassadors to the Duke of Milan, elected an ambassador to go to the Count of Savoy, sent another to Venice and, generally, took a number of measures useful for the welfare of our Republic. Our notary was Ser Antonio di Ser Michele de Ricavo. We also launched the big galleys.[49]

On 14 September 1422, I resolved to pardon Fibindacci Ricasoli and all others who had harmed me. Through the mediation of Guidaccio Pecori, I made peace with Pandolfo Ricasoli in the presence of the Signoria. He undertook, in his own name and in those of his brothers, sons, grandsons, and relatives, to treat me and my brother, sons, and grandsons as friends, etc. I made a like promise to him in the name of my brother, sons, and grandsons. I have recorded this here so that you, my brothers and grandsons, may observe my wishes and so I command you to do.[50]

[49] These galley fleets were sent to the Levant and to the North Sea ports. By means of these fleets, Florence hoped to establish itself as a maritime power, and to strengthen its position as a center of international commerce.
[50] Pitti was alive in 1430, but he was dead when the city's third *catasto* survey was made in 1433; *ASF, Catasto*, 395, fols. 79v–80v; 489, fols. 358v–359v.

The Diary of Gregorio Dati

IN the name of God, his Mother and all the Saints of
Paradise, I shall begin this book wherein I shall set
forth an account of our activities so as to have a record of
them, and wherein having once more and always invoked
the name of God, I shall record the secret affairs of our
company and their progress from year to year. This ledger
belongs to Goro [Gregorio], son of Stagio Dati, and I
shall call it the secret ledger. In the name of God, Father,
Son, and Holy Ghost, I shall here record some particular
things known to myself. God grant they meet with the
approval of whoever learns of them when I am gone.

I learn from old registers that Dato and Pero di Bencivenni were purse-vendors on the Ponte Vecchio next to
the fishmongers, and that their shop was destroyed by the
flood of 1333. It appears from there that Dato had a
number of sons, the eldest of whom, Stagio, was born on 9
March 1317. His mother's name was Monna Filippa. According to Stagio's registers he married our mother, Monna
Ghita, in the year . . . , giving her the the ring on 5
August and celebrating the wedding on 4 November.

I find that Stagio went into partnership with Vanni di Ser
Lotto [Castellani]. The company was set up on 1 January
1353 with a capital of one thousand gold florins. This appears on page 3 of Register A.

I was born on 15 April 1362. This is recorded in a register marked with an asterisk on page 85 where the seventeen
children he had by Monna Ghita are listed in order of age.

·   ·   ·

Our father Stagio left this world for a better one on 11 September 1374, when he was a Consul of the Wool Guild and Treasurer of the Commission on the Salt Tax and Forced Loans. He had been ill for several days before his death and, several days earlier, while still in health, had made a will. He received all the sacraments of the church as befits a devout Christian, and by the mercy of God passed on to eternal life in a state of grace.

On 15 April 1375, when I had learned enough arithmetic, I went to work in the silk merchant's shop belonging to Giovanni di Giano and his partners. I was thirteen years old and I won their esteem.

We gave Madalena [Goro's sister] in marriage in June 1380. This is recorded in register E, page 84.

I left Giovanni di Giano on 2 October 1380, spent fifteen months with the Wool Guild and returned to him on 1 January 1382.

. . .

Partnership Accounts— 1384

In the name of God, the Virgin Mary and all the Saints —may they grant me health in soul and body and prosperity in business—I shall record here all my dealings with our company.

On 1 January 1385, Giovanni di Giano and his partners made me a partner in their silk business for as long as it may please God. I am to invest 300 gold florins which I have not got, being actually in debt to the business. However, with God's help, I hope to have the money shortly and am to receive two out of every twenty-four shares, in other words, a twelfth of the total profit. We settled our accounts on 8 June 1387, on Giovanni di Giano's death. May he rest in peace. My share of the profits for the two years and five months I had been a partner came to 468 gold florins, 7 *soldi a fiorino*.[1] Thanks be to God. We

[1] The phrase *soldi a fiorino* refers to a money of account commonly used in Florentine monetary calculation. Twenty-nine *soldi a fiorino* were equivalent to one gold florin.

formed a new partnership on the following terms: Buonaccorso Berardi is to invest 8,000 florins and have eleven shares; Michele di Ser Parente is to invest 3,500 florins and have eight shares; Goro, son of Stagio Dati, is to invest 500 florins and have three shares; Nardo di Lippo is to invest 500 and have two shares. Thus the capital of the company shall amount to 12,500 gold florins. And if any partner invests additional money in the company, that investment will earn one-half of the percentage of the profits earned by the regular shares.

On 1 January 1389, we settled our accounts, and my share of the profits for the nineteen months came to 552 gold florins, 6 *soldi a fiorino*. Praise and thanks be to God. On 1 January 1390, we reviewed our accounts for the year and my profit was 341 florins, 10 *soldi a fiorino*. Thanks be to God. I left for Valencia on the company's business on 1 September 1390 and got there on 26 October. I was back in Florence on 29 November 1392. The accounts I kept regarding our business there is entered in the white ledger on page . . . in my name and Berardo's. The company did not pay any of our expenses for this trip. It is true that Giovanni left the business in a bad way and with a number of debts.

On 1 January 1393, we dissolved the company and Michele di Ser Parente withdrew all his investments. My profit was reckoned as 1,416 florins, 21 *soldi a fiorino,* and 60 florins were paid for Simone's salary. However this was assuming Giovanni Stefani's debt would be paid, which it has not been, and so it was decided instead that 954 florins, 25 *soldi a fiorino* cash should be deducted from my account corresponding to the debts outstanding, and that I should get back this money when the debts were paid. This was done in order to enable us to set up a new company with real money. Anyway, between cash and expectations my profits came to 1,476 florins, 21 *soldi a fiorino*.

Recommending ourselves to God and good fortune, we set up a new company for a year, starting on 1 January 1393 on the following terms: Buonaccorso Berardi shall invest 4,000 florins and receive eleven shares; Goro di Stagio shall invest 1,000 florins and receive five shares; Nardo di Lippo shall invest 500 florins and receive three and one-half shares; Bernardo di Giovanni shall invest 500 florins and receive three and one-half shares. The capital shall amount to 6,000 florins. May the Lord bless our enterprise.

.   .   .

In God's name I shall continue my review of the accounts written above on page two of our company's agreements, and of my shares, balance sheets and profits and shall re-cord what followed and is yet to follow. As appears in these accounts, we renewed our partnership on 1 January 1393 when I undertook to invest 1,000 florins. I did not actually have the money but was about to get married— which I then did—and to receive the dowry which procured me a larger share and more consideration in our company. Yet we achieved little that year.

I set out for Valencia in September 1393 in order to wind up matters there but did not get beyond Genoa. When I reached the Riviera, I was set upon and robbed by a galley from Briganzone and returned to Florence on 14 December, having lost 250 florins' worth of pearls, mer-chandise and clothes belonging to myself, and 300 gold florins' worth of the company's property.

On 1 January 1394, we drew up our balance sheet and my profit came to 162 florins, 2 *soldi a fiorino*. We renewed our partnership for another year and made a few changes. Whereas Buonaccorso Berardi had previously invested 4,000 florins and received eleven shares, under the new arrangement he was to invest 4,000 florins and receive twelve shares, and whereas I had previously invested 1,000 florins and received five shares, I was now to invest 500 florins and receive four shares. The reason for this was that I had not got the money and Antonio di Segna put it

up. (In this agreement "this year" is to be read as "last
year" and "Buonaccorso Berardi" is to be understood as
including Antonio di Segna, who is to be paid what is due
to him by Buonaccorso at the latter's discretion.)

I went to Valencia on 20 April 1394 and returned on 24
January of the next year. On 1 February 1395, our company expired and we settled our accounts. My profit was
295 florins, and Simone's salary for the outgoing year was
30 florins. May God be thanked. That December I left
Simone in Valencia with Andrea Lopis who was to invest
500 florins in Simone's name on the understanding that all
profits on cloth, silks, and other matters were to be divided
equally between them and that any goods they might order
from me for their own use were to be paid for within the
usual time, six months. Moreover, I was to send them goods
of my own and they were to sell them for me and take a
commission.

On January 1396, I found I had made 600 florins on my
own, independently of any partnership, on goods sent to
and received from Valencia and elsewhere. My expenditure,
however, of which I have kept no account, came to about
250 florins, leaving a balance of 350. These sums, earned
over three years in the three payments mentioned above,
are entered like the others on page 2[2] above. Altogether I
found myself in 1395 with little cash in hand, as a result of
the great expenses to which I had gone in the hope that
they would yield greater profits than they did. In addition,
there were the expenses I was put to by our brother Don
Jacopo,[3] my losses over Giovanni Stefani in Valencia, and
the money which was stolen from me near Genoa. It is fit-
ting to give praise to God for all things. Altogether, having
reckoned my profits, the two dowries received and my outlay for the half-share in the farm in S. Andrea, bought from
Monna Tita, I have about 200 florins in hand. God grant
that henceforth we prosper in soul and body. This balance

[2] These and other page references refer to pages in Dati's ledger.
[3] Jacopo was a priest.

of 200 florins is entered on page 3 above under Receipt and Expenditure.

Memoranda, 1393

In God's name, I shall continue this record of my activities, which it is well to have in writing so as to recollect them, and which I began back on page 1. My beloved wife, Bandecca, went to Paradise after a nine-month illness started by a miscarriage in the fifth month of pregnancy. It was eleven o'clock at night on Friday, 15 July 1390, when she peacefully returned her soul to her Creator in Buonaccorso Berardi's house. The next day I had her buried in S. Brancazio; she had received the last sacraments.

I went to Valencia on 1 September 1390, taking Bernardo with me. I came back on 30 November 1392, having suffered much hardship during my stay, both in mind and body. We were still owed 4,000 Barcelona pounds by Giovanni di Stefano, who acknowledged this debt in a notarized deed which I brought back with me to Florence. In Valencia I had an illegitimate male child by Margherita, a Tartar slave whom I had bought. He was born on 21 December 1391, in Valencia on St. Thomas's Day and I named him after that saint. I sent him to Florence in March on Felice del Pace's ship. God grant that he turn out well.

On the expiration of our partnership, on 1 January 1393, Michele di Ser Parente withdrew. Later, I made an agreement with him whereby he made over to me his share in Giovanni di Stefani's debt and a few other items which are entered on page 6.

I married my second wife, Isabetta, the daughter of Mari Vilanuzzi on Sunday, 22 June, as is recorded on the other side of this page.

On 10 September 1393, I left Florence for Catalonia and, while we were at sea in a small galley a little beyond Portovenere, a galley from Briganzone came after us, held us up, and robbed us and took our goods to Baldo Spinoli at Briganzone. We got some of them back later, although with great difficulty and at great expense. I came back here on 14 December. On 20 April, I went to Valencia on Felice's ship. I visited Majorca and Barcelona where Simone joined me, after which we both went to Valencia where I left him. I returned home by land and reached Florence on 24 January 1395. Thanks be to God. Our partnership expired on 1 February 1395, and that year I did business of my own and was very successful. Thanks be to God. I went into partnership once more with Michele di Ser Parente on 1 January 1396, and the terms and clauses are entered on page 6.

Our Simone, who had been in Valencia since December 1394, wanted to come to Florence. He arrived on 12 December 1396, and left to go back there on 3 January 1397. However, while he was at sea, a Neapolitan galley overtook him just outside Pisa and took him as a prisoner to Naples. On 3 April, he was released for ransom at Gaeta, from whence he made his way back to Valencia.

A general remission and acquittance was granted to us, to Michele di Ridolfo's sons, and to the Commune of Florence with regard to the matter concerning Dato by Andrea da Bologna, an inhabitant of Montpellier, on 14 February 1398. The notary was Giovanni da Pino. This is entered in my long Ledger A, page 131. It cost us 100 gold francs and I have the deed in my strong-box.[4]

My Wife Betta's Personal Accounts—1393

In the name of God and the Virgin Mary, of Blessed Michael the Archangel, of SS. John the Baptist and John the Evangelist, of SS. Peter and Paul, of the holy scholars, SS. Gregory and Jerome, and of St. Mary Magdalene and St. Elisabeth and all the blessed saints in heaven—may they ever intercede for us—I shall record here how I married my second wife, Isabetta, known as Betta, the daughter of Mari di Lorenzo Vilanuzzi and of Monna Veronica, daugh-

[4] This was apparently an old business dispute involving Gregorio Dati's grandfather, Dato.

ter of Pagolo d'Arrigo Guglielmi, and I shall also record the promises which were made to me. May God and his Saints grant by their grace that they be kept.

On 31 March 1393, I was betrothed to her and on Easter Monday, 7 April, I gave her the ring. On 22 June, a Sunday, I became her husband in the name of God and good fortune. Her first cousins, Giovanni and Lionardo di Domenico Arrighi, promised that she should have a dowry of 900 gold florins and that, apart from the dowry, she should have the income on a farm in S. Fiore a Elsa, which had been left her as a legacy by her mother, Monna Veronica. It was not stated at the time how much this amounted to, but it was understood that she would receive the accounts. We arranged our match very simply indeed and with scarcely any discussion. God grant that nothing but good may come of it. On the 26th of that same June, I received a payment of 800 gold florins from the bank of Giacomino and Company. This was the dowry. I invested it in the shop of Buonaccorso Berardi and his partners, and it is recorded here, on page 2 among the profits. At the same time I received the trousseau which my wife's cousins valued at 106 florins, in the light of which they deducted six florins from another account, leaving me the equivalent of 100 gold florins. But from what I heard from her and what I saw myself, they had overestimated it by 30 florins or more. However, from politeness, I said nothing about this.

I have not declared this dowry nor insured it on account of their negligence and in order to put off paying the tax. They dare not urge me to do so since they are obligated towards me. Yet I must do so, and if by God's will something were to happen before I do, I want her to be as assured as can be of having her dowry, just as though it had been declared and insured. For the fault is not hers. It turns out that the income she is to receive comes from a farm in S. Fiore on the Elsa on the way to Pisa. It is a nice piece of property which apparently belonged to Pagolo Guglielmi. Giovanni and Lionardo bought it from Betta's mother, Monna Veronica, or rather bought a half-share in it for 500 gold florins and paid a tax on this sale. Later they sold back their share to Monna Veronica, paying another tax, for 575 florins. These transactions are recorded in the register of taxes on contracts in register 500, 40; 500, 41 and 500, 42. When Monna Veronica died in April 1391, she left the income from this farm to Betta and to her children after her.

On 26 September 1402, as Simone was in Florence for a while before leaving for Catalonia, and as the penalties for evading the tax on contracts were remitted by law for those who paid that day, I and Simone declared the dowry of 900 gold florins received from Leonardo and Domenico. The notary was Ser Giunta Franceschi and on the 30th of the same September, I paid 30 gold florins, being 3⅓ per cent, to the account of the taxes on contracts.

Our Lord God was pleased to call to himself the blessed soul of Isabetta, known as Betta, on Monday, 2 October, between four and five o'clock in the afternoon. The next day, Tuesday, at three in the afternoon, she was buried in our grave at S. Spirito. May God receive her soul in His glory. Amen.

Children, 1393

In praise, glory, honor and benediction of Almighty God, I shall record the fruits that His grace will grant us, and may He in His mercy vouchsafe that they be such as to console our souls eternally, amen. On Sunday morning, 17 May 1394, Betta gave birth to a girl whom we called Bandecca in memory of my first wife. Goro d'Andrea, Niccolaio di Bartolommeo Niccoli, and Berardo di Buonacorso were her sponsors.

On Friday evening, 17 March 1396, towards two o'clock in the morning, the Lord blessed our marriage with a male son whom we named Stagio and whom we had baptized in the love of God on Sunday morning by Fra Simone Bartoli of the Augustinian Hermits, my partner Nardo di Lippo, and Sandro di Jacopo, a pauper.

At two o'clock in the night of Monday, 12 March 1397, Betta gave birth to our third child, a girl. We called her after Betta's mother, giving her the names Veronica Gostanza, and Sandro di Jacopo baptized her in the love of God.

At midday on Saturday, 27 April 1398, Betta gave birth to our fourth child which was a boy. We called him Bernardo Agostino and he was baptized the same day in the love of God by Monna Agnola del Ciri and Monna Francesca Aldobrandino. God grant he turn out well.

At dawn on Tuesday, 1 July 1399, Betta had our fifth child and we baptized him in the love of God the same day, calling him Mari Piero. The sponsors were Master Lionardo[5] and Fra Zanobi.

On Tuesday evening, 22 June 1400, Betta gave birth for the sixth time. The child was a girl. We called her Filippa Giovanna and she was baptized on Friday morning in the love of God. Fra Simone Bartoli held her.

Our Lord God was pleased to take to Himself the fruits which He had lent us, and He took first our most beloved, Stagio, our darling and blessed first-born. He died of the plague on the morning of Friday, 30 July 1400, in Florence without my seeing him, for I was in the country. Master Lionardo and Monna Ghita were with him. May God bless him and grant that he pray for us.

On 22 August of the same year, the Divine bounty was pleased to desire a companion for that beloved soul. God called our son Mari to Himself and he died at eleven o'clock on Sunday, of the plague. God grant us the grace to find favor with Him and to bless and thank Him for all things.

On Wednesday, 13 July 1401, after midnight, the Lord lent us a seventh child. Betta had a son who we called Stagio Benedetto. The sponsors were Nardo di Lippo and Domenico Benini. Divine providence was pleased to take him back and for this too may He be thanked and praised. The child suffered from a cough for a fortnight, and at

[5] Gregorio's brother, Lionardo Dati, was a Dominican friar, who later was elected General of the Order.

midday on 29 September, St. Michael's Day and the Eve
of St. Jerome's Day, passed away to Paradise. God grant
that we, when we leave this mortal life, may follow him
there.

On 5 July 1402, before the hour of terce, Betta gave
birth to our eighth child. We had him baptized straight
after terce in the love of God. His godparents were Nardo
and blind Margherita, and we called him Piero Antonio
because of Betta's special devotion to S. Antonio. God
bless him and grant that he become a good man.

After that my wife Isabetta passed on to Paradise as is
recorded on the opposite page, and I shall have no more
children by her to list here. God be praised.

Our Creator was pleased to call to Himself the soul of
our gentle and good son Antonio. He left this life, I think,
on 2 August. For I was in great trouble and did not know
it at the time. It was in Pisa where he is buried at S.
Caterina's.

Betta and I had eight children, five boys and three
girls.

Memo, 1394

I record that on 1 February I withdrew from the partnership with Buonacorso Berardi and did business on my
own this year. I bought goods and sent them to Simone in
Valencia, lent money to friends in Pisa and elsewhere,
received goods from Valencia for sale here and continued
like this for eight months until the beginning of October. I
did very well during this period. I have not kept accounts
but earned and spent on my own. Yet I can see that the
transactions I carried out have been successful, and I hope
those which are not yet concluded will be equally so. I may
go through with them by myself or may go into partnership with someone.

And once more in God's name I have formed a partnership with Michele di Ser Parente from 1 October 1395. In
our account books, it will be reckoned as beginning on 1

January 1396, when Mariotto di Lodovico is to withdraw.
I am now beginning to do things for this new partnership.
I shall record the terms and clauses of our agreements
further on, on page 6, and may God bless our enterprise.

Going over my accounts, I find that when Michele di Ser
Parente withdrew from our partnership on 1 January 1393,
my total assets amounted to about 800 florins, which was
all the actual money I would have possessed had I wished
to withdraw in my turn. This meant I had made no profit.
For I had to pay back about 950 florins which was the part
of my profits corresponding to the debts owed us in Catalonia and elsewhere, which should not have been reckoned
as recoverable for the moment. We realized this later when
Antonio di Segna's guile made it seem advisable to check
the various assets of the company. This was why I resolved
to put up with anything for the next two years and to stay
in their shop and suffer Antonio di Segna and everything
else, as I was too short of money to try and do things my
own way. I have been hoping that Matteo will help me to
send Simone to Valencia where he will be very useful to me
for my business here. I pray God that it may so turn out.

After that in 1393 I got the dowry which came to 800
florins, while my profits from our partnership were 162
florins, and for the year after were 325 florins which comes
to a total of 1,287 florins. My expenditure, entered in folio
3 under "Expenditure," was in two amounts, totaling
1,425 florins. This includes my losses when I was robbed
on the Riviera, about 275 florins paid for the farm and
about 100 florins lent to Michele's heir. Whereas in 1392
I was owed 950 florins and owed about 150 florins, since
then I find my debits exceeding my credits by about 140
florins, which makes a total debit of 290. I estimate that in
the eight months I have been in business on my own, I have
made good my losses and wiped out this debt, or will have
done so when the ventures I embarked on then have been
concluded. So now I can live within my capital. Would to
God and the Virgin Mary that I were sure of continuing
to do so from 1 January 1396, and were sure that my debits

would not exceed my credits from the time I go into partnership with Michele. But God will grant us His grace as He
has always done. I am not entering the 950 florins and 25
soldi a fiorino in my accounts since they cannot be put to
any use.

After that year by God's grace I did better than I had
expected, for the Valencia branch did well and paid up, and
I have been able to transfer 200 florins from the credit
side and deduct them from my debits as appears on Outgo,
folio 3.

. . .

Account Book—1395

May God and His gentle Mother bestow their grace
upon us. In their name I shall note here the terms and
clauses of the new partnership which I and others formed
with Michele di Ser Parente and the sums of money involved. Michele di Ser Parente shall invest 8,000 florins
and receive thirteen and three-quarter shares; I, Goro di
Stagio, am to invest 1,000 florins and have four and one-
half shares; Nardo di Lippo Nardi is to invest 400 florins
and have two shares. The total capital is to amount to
9,600 florins and be divided in twenty-four shares.[6]

I engage to contribute 1,000 florins to the capital of our
partnership so as to enjoy a substantial share and consideration in the firm. I have not got the cash at present but expect
that Matteo di Tommaso will lend me 400 florins belonging to his stepmother, Monna Lorenza, plus some money
of his own. I shall try to raise the rest somewhere else if I
can and will debit it to the Valencia account until I have
made enough either in my business here or with Simone in
Valencia to pay it back.

I have agreed with Michele to send his son Giovanni to

---

[6] The disparity between capital invested and shares held is due to the fact
that some partners (e.g., Michele di Ser Parente) contributed capital and
no labor, while others (Dati, Spinello, and Niccolaio del Bene) contributed
their services as part of their investment in the company.

Valencia, where he is to form a business partnership with Simone for as long as we shall decide. We will supply the goods they require and our firm will put 1,000 florins cash at their disposal. One half of whatever profits they make will be ours, and the other half is to be divided between them, so that each will have one quarter of the total profits. Giovanni went to Valencia in May 1396, but only stayed there a short time as he did not get on with Simone. Simone came to Florence on 12 December 1396 and reached an agreement with myself and Michele whereby they were to keep whatever profits, good or bad, they might manage to make in Valencia, without giving our firm any share in them, and to pay us whatever they owed us on the usual terms.

Simone left here for Valencia on 3 January and, having set sail from Pisa on the 8th, was captured by one of King Louis's[7] admirals, Messer Giovanni Gonsalvo of Seville, who took him as a prisoner to Naples. When he had been held there for three months, he was taken to Gaeta and released for a ransom of 200 florins. This was paid for him by Doffo Spini, whom we reimbursed, and debited to the Valencia account with a number of other expenses. On 3 April, he left for Majorca on the *nave dipungiata*.[8] May God grant he get there safely and that we recover our losses. Giovanni and Simone continued to wrangle and bicker even more than before, until finally Giovanni resolved to leave for Barcelona and settle there. They continued, however, to be partners. Then of their own accord they dissolved the partnership, agreeing that Simone should keep whatever profits he had made in Valencia and Giovanni should have what he had made in Barcelona. God grant His grace to each of them.

Shop Accounts, 1403

When the partnership with Michele di Ser Parente expired, I set up shop on my own under the name of Goro

[7] Louis of Anjou, claimant to the Kingdom of Naples.
[8] *nave dipungiata*. The phrase should perhaps be translated: "the ship owned [or captained] by Pungiata."

Stagio and company. My partners are Piero and Jacopo di Tommaso Lana who contribute 3,000 [florins] while I contribute 2,000, and Nardo di Lippo who contributes his services. The partnership is to start on 1 January 1403 and to last three years. The clauses and articles of agreement and the amounts invested by each partner will be entered in a secret ledger covered with white leather belonging to our partnership.

On my own account and with my own money, I paid 75 florins to the heirs of Simone Vespucci and their representative, Lapo Vespucci, for the goodwill and licence to exercise my profession in one of the shops of Por Santa Maria.[9] The brokers were Andrea di Bonaventura and Niccolaio Niccoli. On 6 March 1403, Isau d'Agnolo and Antonio Manni, a silk merchant who was in the shop, received 25 florins from me. The broker was Meo d'Andrea del Benino. The fixtures and repairs cost me about 100 florins, so altogether, between the goodwill and the fixtures I paid 200 florins out of my own pocket, in God's name, for myself and my heirs. The site of the shop belongs to the Carthusian monks, from whom I am to rent it on the usual terms for 35 gold florins a year. Ser Ludovico of the guild drew up the lease, which is to run for five years from the beginning of February 1403.

As already stated, I have undertaken to put up 2,000 florins. This is how I propose to raise them: 1,370 florins and 25 *soldi a fiorino* are still due to me from my old partnership with Michele di Ser Parente, as appears on page 118 of my ledger for stock and cash on hand. The rest I expect to obtain if I marry again this year, when I hope to find a woman with a dowry as large as God may be pleased to grant me. If I do not marry, I will find the money some other way.

The partnership with Piero was set up and formally notarized several months ago. Voluntarily and of his own accord, he asked me to see to the investments and the dividing into shares, leaving all this in my hands. The articles

[9] Por Santa Maria was the guild of the silk manufacturers.

of our agreement are entered in my long ledger on page 163 and the sums I have received or am to receive from him are entered on page 164 and the following pages. I intend to transfer this entry to the secret ledger which I plan to keep of our partnership's affairs, so that it may not be mentioned or entered in any other registers. I think I will get as much as 3,000 florins from him so as to avoid having to divide our profits with too many others. I hope to put his investments and my own to good use if our trade with Valencia is successful, which may God grant. Piero and I are agreed that Nardo di Lippo should be a partner and have a share in the profits to which he is entitled, although he need not invest money in our enterprise, as he has not got any. He is to pay me the money which he has coming to him from Michele's shop and more.

After the last entry, on 4 July 1403, I invested Ginevra's dowry in our company. As appears further on on page 8, it came to 671 florins. I entered this in the secret ledger. At the beginning of January 1404, I examined my accounts and found that I had made excellent profits. However, I did not close our accounts as a large shipment of goods was at sea on its way to Simone.

In that year, 1404, Simone and the King of Castile became involved in the business of the Venetian customs. He needed a great deal of goods from us and much of what we sent him we had to buy. Later, as a result of the King of Aragon's laws directed against anyone shipping goods to the King of Castile,[10] this merchandise was held up in Barcelona. Antonio Gucci, who was there for the Serristori and was also looking after our interests, had a run of bad luck and tried to make us suffer for losses which were not ours, so that we found ourselves involved in litigation over this with the Serristori in Florence. The case went to the Merchants' Court, and consequently, I lost credit and suffered much damage. Nonetheless, I drew up a fresh balance sheet in January 1405, and found that I had earned

[10] The quarreling monarchs were Martin of Aragon (1395–1410) and Henry III of Castile (1390–1406).

good profits thanks to Simone's credit. Once more we did not close our accounts as there were only two of us, but the lawsuit over the dissensions begun in September 1405 went from bad to worse for us.

My Wife Ginevra's Accounts—1403

In the name of God and of the Virgin Mary, may His help be with us at the beginning, middle and end of every enterprise. I shall write here about my third wife and her affairs.

I record that on 8 May 1403, I was betrothed to Ginevra, daughter of Antonio di Piero Piuvichese Brancacci, in S. Maria sopra Porta. The dowry was 1,000 florins: 700 in cash and 300 in a farm at Campi. On Saturday morning, S. Stagio's Day, 20 May, we were married, but we held no festivities nor wedding celebrations as we were in mourning for Manetto Dati who had died the week before. God grant us a good life together. Ginevra had been married before for four years to Tommaso Brancacci, by whom she had an eight-month old son. She is now in her twenty-first year. Bartolo di Giovanni di Niccola promised to let me have the dowry by the end of next June.

On 4 July of that year, in the house which formerly belonged to Manetto Dati, I received the dowry from Felice di Michele Brancacci who sent it to me by Ser Giovanni d'Andrea da Linari. It consisted of 700 gold florins in cash and a farm, of which the value was not assessed, situated in Campi, at a place called *a l'Oliva* or *al Trebio*, of about 52 *staiori*.[11] It is bounded on three sides by the road and on the fourth by the monastery of S. Giovanni, which is attached to S. Felice in Piazza.[12] I, Monna Ghita, Stagio di Manetto, Nardo di Lippo and myself a second time as Simone's legal representative, declared and insured the

[11] A *staiora* was an area of land that could be sown by one *staio* (approximately a bushel) of grain.
[12] S. Felice in Piazza was a monastery of the Sylvestrine Order (after 1413, the Camaldoli) located in Florence on the south side of the Arno.

dowry and I got the money from Bartolo or rather from his company, that of Lorenzo di Dinozo, through the bank of Averardo. It amounted to 671 florins in cash and a trousseau worth 29 florins.

. . .

1 January 1404.

I know that in this wretched life our sins expose us to many tribulations of soul and passions of the body, that without God's grace and mercy which strengthens our weakness, enlightens our mind and supports our will, we would perish daily. I also see that since my birth forty years ago, I have given little heed to God's commandments. Distrusting my own power to reform, but hoping to advance by degrees along the path of virtue, I resolve from this day forward to refrain from going to the shop or conducting business on solemn Church holidays, or from permitting others to work for me or seek temporal gain on such days. Whenever I make exceptions in cases of extreme necessity, I promise, on the following day, to distribute alms of one gold florin to God's poor. I have written this down so that I may remember my promise and be ashamed if I should chance to break it.

Also, in memory of the passion of Our Lord Jesus Christ who freed and saved us by His merits, that He may, by His grace and mercy preserve us from guilty passions, I resolve from this very day and in perpetuity to keep Friday as a day of total chastity—with Friday I include the following night—when I must abstain from the enjoyment of all carnal pleasures. God give me grace to keep my promise, yet if I should break it through forgetfulness, I engage to give 20 *soldi* to the poor for each time, and to say twenty Paternosters and Avemarias.

I resolve this day to do a third thing while I am in health and able to, remembering that each day we need Almighty God to provide for us. Each day I wish to honor God by some giving of alms or by the recitation of prayers or some other pious act. If, by inadvertence, I fail to do so, that day or the next day I must give alms to God's poor of at least 5 *soldi*. These however are not vows but intentions by which I shall do my best to abide.[13]

3 May 1412. On 28 April, my name was drawn as Standard-bearer of the Militia Company.[14] Up until then I had not been sure whether my name was in the purses for that office, although I was eager that it should be both for my own honor and that of my heirs. I recalled that my father Stagio had held a number of appointments in the course of his life, being frequently a consul of the Guild of Por Santa Maria, a member of the Merchants' Court and one of the officials in charge of gabelles and the treasurers. Yet he was never drawn for any of the Colleges during his lifetime, though shortly after his death he was drawn as a prior. I recalled that I had aroused a great deal of animosity eight years ago because of my business in Catalonia, and that last year I only just escaped being arrested for debt by the Commune. On the very day my name was drawn for this office, only fifteen minutes before it was drawn, I had taken advantage of the reprieve granted by the new laws and finished paying off my debt to the Commune. That was a veritable inspiration from God, may His name be praised and blessed! Now that I can obtain other offices, it seems to me that, having had a great benefit, I should be content to know that I have sat once in the Colleges and should aspire no further. So, lest I should ungratefully give way to the insatiable appetites of those in whom success breeds renewed ambition, I have resolved and sworn to myself that I shall not henceforth invoke the aid of any or attempt to get myself elected to public offices or to have my name included in new purses. Rather, I shall let things take their course without interfering. I shall abide by God's will, accepting those offices of the guilds or Commune for which my name shall be drawn, and not refusing the labor but serving and doing what good I may. In this way I shall

---

[13] Dati meant that these obligations were not to be considered legally binding.
[14] A member of one of the Signoria's advisory Colleges. Dati's district (*gonfalone*) was Ferze, in the quarter of S. Spirito.

restrain my own presumption and tendency towards ambition and shall live in freedom without demeaning myself
by begging favors from any. And if I should depart from
this resolve, I condemn myself each time to distribute two
gold florins in alms within a month. I have taken this resolution in my fiftieth year.

Knowing my weakness in the face of sin, I make another
resolve on the same day. In order to ensure the peace and
good of my own conscience, I vowed that I would never
accept any office, if my name should be drawn, wherein I
would have power to wield the death penalty. If I should
depart from this resolution, I condemn myself to give 25
gold florins in alms to the poor within three months for each
such office that I have agreed to accept. And I shall in no
way attempt to influence those who make up the purses for
such offices, either asking them to put or not put in my
name, but shall let them do as they think fit. If I should do
otherwise, I condemn myself to distribute a gold florin.

Children—1404

Glory, honor and praise be to Almighty God. Continuing
from folio 5, I shall list the children which He shall in His
grace bestow on me and my wife, Ginevra.

On Sunday morning at terce, 27 April of the same year,
Ginevra gave birth to our first-born son. He was baptized
at the hour of vespers on Monday the 28th in the church
of S. Giovanni. We named him Manetto Domenico. His
sponsors in God's love were Bartolo di Giovanni di Niccola,
Giovanni di Michelozzo, a belt-maker, and Domenico di
Deo, a goldsmith. God make him good.

At the third hour of Thursday, 19 March 1405, Ginevra
gave birth to a female child of less than seven months. She
had not realized she was pregnant, since for four months
she had been ailing as though she were not, and in the end
was unable to hold it. We baptized it at once in the church
of S. Giovanni. The sponsors were Bartolo, Monna Buona,
another lady, and the blind woman. Having thought at first

that it was a boy, we named it Agnolo Giovanni. It died at dawn on Sunday morning, 22 March, and was buried before the sermon.

At terce on Tuesday morning, 8 June 1406, Ginevra had her third child, a fine full-term baby girl whom we had baptized on Friday morning, 9 June. We christened her Elisabetta Caterina and she will be called Lisabetta in memory of my dead wife, Betta. The sponsors were Fra Lorenzo, Bartolo, and the blind woman.

On 4 June 1407, a Saturday, Ginevra gave birth after a nine-month pregnancy to a little girl whom we had baptized on the evening of Tuesday the 7th. We named her Antonia Margherita and we shall call her Antonia. Her godfather was Nello di Ser Piero Nelli, a neighbor. God grant her good fortune.

At terce, Sunday, 31 July 1411, Ginevra gave birth to a very attractive baby boy whom we had baptized on 4 August. The sponsors were my colleagues among the Standard-bearers of the Militia Companies with the exception of two: Giorgio and Bartolomeo Fioravanti. We called the child Niccolò. God bless him. God was pleased to call the child very shortly to Himself. He died of dysentery on 22 October at terce. May he intercede with God for us.

At terce on Sunday, 1 October 1412, Ginevra had a son whom, from devotion to St. Jerome—since it was yesterday that her pains began—I called Girolamo Domenico. The sponsors were Master Bartolomeo del Carmine, Cristofano di Francesco di Ser Giovanni, and Lappuccio di Villa, and his son Bettino. God grant him and us health and make him a good man.

God willed that the blessed soul of our daughter Betta should return to Him after a long illness. She passed away during the night between Tuesday and the first Wednesday of Lent at four in the morning, 21 February 1414. She was seven years and seven months, and I was sorely grieved at her death. God grant she pray for us.

On 1 May 1415, at the hour of terce on a Wednesday, God granted us a fine little boy, and I had him baptized at four on Saturday morning. Jacopo di Francesco di Tura and Aringhieri di Jacopo, the wool merchant, were his godfathers. May God grant that he be healthy, wise, and good. We named him after the two holy apostles, Jacopo and Filippo, on whose feast day he was born and we shall call him Filippo.

At eleven o'clock on Friday, 24 April 1416, Ginevra gave birth to a baby girl after a painful and almost fatal labor. The child was baptized immediately on S. Marco's Day, the 25th. We called her Ghita in memory of our mother. Monna Mea di Franchino was her godmother.

Manetto died in Pisa in January 1418. He had been very sick and was buried in S. Martino. Pippo died on 2 August 1419 in Val di Pesa in a place called Polonia. This is recorded in notebook B.

At two o'clock on the night following Monday 17 July, Lisa was born. She was baptized by Master Pagolo from Montepulciano, a preaching friar,[15] on Wednesday at seven o'clock. God console us, amen. She later died.

Altogether Ginevra and I had eleven children: four boys and seven girls.

Memorandum—1405

To take up my record of past years from folio 7, I served among the Ten on Liberty.[16] My term began on 1 April and ran four months. My colleagues were Arrigo Mazinghi, Niccoloso Cambi, Giraldo di Lorenzo, Piero Velluti, Nastagio di Benincasa, Uguccione Giandonati, Michele di Banco, two artisans, and myself. I pleased everyone and acted as rightly as I was able.

I was Guild Consul for the third time from 1 May of the same year. With me were Zanobi di Ser Gino, Agnolo di Ghezzo, Noze Manetti, and Agnolo di Filippo di Ser Giovanni [Pandolfini].

[15] A member of the Dominican Order.
[16] The Ten on Liberty (*Dieci di Libertà*) was a magistracy whose primary function was to settle quarrels between citizens.

I began proceedings against Messer Giovanni Serristori and Company on the . . . of September before the Merchants' Court. I was reluctant to do this but had no choice. I had suffered grievous harm in spirit and pocket and was likely to be ruined if I did not defend myself. God bring me safely out of this! The partnership with Piero and Jacopo Lana and Nardo di Lippo expired on 31 December 1406. We did not renew it because of the risks we had run in connection with what had happened in Spain. It is advisable for us to lie low for a while and wait and pay our creditors and put our trust in God. I have reached an agreement with Piero establishing the time and manner in which I must pay him. I am to do so through Bernardo who has a copy of the agreement.

I was a Guild Consul for the fourth time from 1 September 1408, in company with Lapo Corsi, Chimento di Stefano, Filippo di Ghezo, Francesco di Messer Jacopo Marchi, and Matteo di Lorenzo, the goldsmith.

On 11 November 1408, I set out for Valencia and Murcia, and reached Murcia on 30 December. I travelled overland in the company of Pagolo Mei and it was a difficult journey. I left Murcia in May 1410 and delayed in Valencia on account of the risks of both the sea and land route, due to the war between ourselves and the King[17] and the Genoese. In February I finally set out and took ship at Barcelona whence I sailed for Piombino which I reached on 12 March at terce on St. Gregory's Day and was in Florence on 15 March 1411.

In that year 1411, there was a plague, and Piero Lana died. That December I made an agreement with his brother and partner, Jacopo, who had been my partner too, and with Piero's sons through Dino di Messer Guccio and Bernardo and Pagolo di Vanni and Zanobi di Ser Benozzo, who acted as intermediaries.

Our Master Lionardo was elected Father General of the Dominican Order by the chapter, with great harmony and

[17] Florence's antagonist was King Ladislaus of Naples. This war is described in Pitti's diary.

festivities and honor on 29 September, the Feast of the
Angels, and the following day, the feast of S. Jerome, the
holiday and procession were held. Praise be to God.

Mona Ghita, our beloved mother, departed this wretched
life and returned her soul to her Creator before dawn on
Monday morning, 29 January 1414. She received the last
sacraments and passed away peacefully. May God receive
her in his bosom. Amen.

. . .

Partnership with Pietro Lana, 1408

The accounts of the shop and company are written above
on page 8. As a result of the adversity which overtook us
in Barcelona, and of the lawsuit here which followed it, and
of the suspicions concerning Simone's ventures and the
calumnies that were spread about, we were very short of
credit. So we were forced to withdraw from business and
collect whatever we could to pay our creditors, borrowing
from friends and using all our ingenuity, suffering losses,
high interest and expense in order to avoid bankruptcy and
shame. And although my partner was in favor of going
bankrupt so as to avoid some losses and expenditure, I was
resolved to face ruin rather than loss of honor. I held out
so firmly and struggled to such purpose that in the end we
managed to pay all our debts, and I satisfied all claims except those of my partners. May God be praised and blessed.
I am sure too that if I had managed to send Simone the silk
and gold which he was to sell the King, he would have
brought his business to a successful conclusion. But I could
not send it, and indeed had to abandon all business activity
until 1405. Then the lawsuit began and I had to sell whatever goods I had here so as to pay my debts, and I was
obliged to renege on my promises to send him what he
needed for the King. Consequently, his business began to
collapse and stagnate. Indeed, it sank into such confusion
that it was been impossible to set it back on its feet, and it
has gone ever since from bad to worse.

As Simone was doing badly himself, he was unable to send us the consignments and remittances we needed. My partner, who had grown very impatient, kept complaining in public and behaving in a way unfavorable to our common interest. While I was in Spain, Antonio di Ser Bartolomeo and two other powerful companies took proceedings against him in connection with a transaction they had concluded with me. He defended our interest very badly, did not produce our accounts as evidence, and merely tried to show that he himself was not liable. The judgement went against him and he was forced to pay. Of the 500 florins we had received from them, I had already paid back 300 florins to their agent in Spain, so that we only owed them a residue of 200. Yet they were awarded 2,000 silver florins. I do not think such a thing ever happened before or since. And I hope it may bring them bad luck. Yet we have to stand to the loss of it and the fault lies with my partner and his crooked ways.

Hearing that Pagolo Mei was going to Spain, I decided to travel with him and see whether I could save something from the ruin of our branch there. We left Florence on 12 November 1408, travelled by land and, after a very wearisome journey in harsh wintry weather, reached Murcia[18] on 30 December. Simone came to meet us there and for a while we had good hopes of his business but these were later deceived because of the falsity of the Spaniards, and because, through no error of his, he was unfairly treated. I was back in Florence safe and sound on 15 March 1411, but all I brought with me was a great deal of sorrow and weariness.

My partner, Lana, kept tormenting me in every way he could and denounced me to the Merchant's Court as a bankrupt, asking them to have me publicly denounced by their herald. He did not succeed in getting them to pass sentence against me, for I had not gone bankrupt but had returned from abroad to settle my accounts with him and to do what

[18] Murcia is an inland town in southeastern Castile, some 100 miles south of the port city of Valencia.

I could towards satisfying him. In the middle of this dispute, he died of the plague in July 1411.

. . .

After that it was God's will to recall to Himself the blessed soul of my wife Ginevra. She died in childbirth after lengthy suffering, which she bore with remarkable strength and patience. She was perfectly lucid at the time of her death when she received all the sacraments: confession, communion, extreme unction, and a papal indulgence granting absolution for all her sins, which she received from Master Lionardo, who had been granted it by the Pope. It comforted her greatly, and she returned her soul to her Creator on 7 September, the Eve of the Feast of Our Lady, at nones: the hour when Our Blessed Lord Jesus Christ expired on the cross and yielded up his spirit to our Heavenly Father. On Friday the 8th she was honorably buried and on the 9th, masses were said for her soul. Her body lies in our plot at S. Spirito and her soul has gone to eternal life. God bless her and grant us fortitude. Her loss has sorely tried me. May He help me to bring up the unruly family which is left to me in the best way for their souls and bodies.

God who shows his wisdom in all things permitted the plague to strike our house. The first to succumb was our manservant Paccino at the end of June 1420. Three days later it was the turn of our slave-girl Marta, after her on 1 July my daughter Sandra and on 5 July my daughter Antonia. We left that house after that and went to live opposite, but a few days later Veronica died. Again we moved, this time to Via Chiara where Bandecca and Pippa fell ill and departed this life on 1 August. All of them bore the marks of the plague. It passed off after that and we returned to our own house. May God bless them all. Bandecca's will and her accounts appear on page . . . of my ledger A.

I then took another wife, Caterina, the daughter of Dardano Guicciardini. She was thirty years of age, and came to our house on 30 March 1421. Her personal accounts are written in detail further on in folio 13. God grant us a good life together, amen.

My name was drawn to serve among the Twelve Good Men, and I began my term of office on 15 September 1421. My colleagues were Antonio d'Ubaldo di Fetto, Buonaccorso Corsellini, Antonio di Piero di Fronte, Piero di Buonaccorso di Vanni, Lapo di Giovanni Bucelli, Dino di Messer Guccio, Tomaso di Giacomo di Goggio, Guarente the goldsmith, Michele di Nardo Pagnini, Bencivenni di Cristoforo, and Puccino di Ser Andrea. No greater unanimity could be found than that which reigned amongst us. Thanks be to God.

My name was drawn to be Overseer for the Guild Hospital [19] for one year. I began to serve on 1 May 1422 with Bartolo Corsi, Giovanni di Deo, Salvi Lotti, Cione di Cecco Cioni, and Tommaso di Pazzino.

On 9 September 1422, the Signoria and Colleges elected me to serve among the Five Defenders of the County and District in lieu of Parigi Corbinelli who had been appointed Podestà. I took office on the 10th of the month and served during January with Giovanni di Messer Forese [Salviati], Salvestro Popoleschi, Giovanni Carradori, and Piero del Palagio. It is an onerous office, in which one may gain merit in the sight of God and acquire contempt for the world. We did a great deal to improve the lot of the unfortunate peasants.

My Fourth Wife's Personal Account

In the name of God and of the Virgin Mary, or SS. Gregory and Catherine. I shall note down here matters relating to my fourth wife.

Memo that on Tuesday, 28 January 1421, I made an agreement with Niccolò d'Andrea del Benino to take his

[19] The famous Spedale degli Innocenti, the Foundling Home in the Piazza SS. Annunziata. The construction of the building, for which Brunelleschi was architect, was begun two years earlier, in 1420.

niece, Caterina, for my lawful wife. She is the daughter of the late Dardano di Niccolò Guicciardini and of Monna Tita, Andrea del Benino's daughter. We were betrothed on the morning of Monday, 3 February, the Eve of Carnival. I met Piero and Giovanni di Messer Luigi [Guicciardini] in the church of S. Maria sopra Porta, and Niccolò d'Andrea del Benino was our mediator. The dowry promised me was 600 florins, and the notary was Ser Niccolò di Ser Verdiano. I went to dine with her that evening in Piero's house and the Saturday after Easter—29 March 1421—Ser Niccolò drew up a public instrument, whereby I attested to the receipt of a dowry amounting to 615 florins from Giovanni di Messer Luigi. I then received it from him and her as appears in my ledger B on page 128, including a trousseau worth fifteen florins. Madalena and Bernardo and Michele di Manetto went surety for me. That day I gave her the ring and then on Sunday evening, 30 March, she came to live in our house simply and without ceremony. On 7 May 1421, I paid the tax on contracts. See Register A 72, page 56. It came to sixteen florins, four *soldi*, four *denari*. God be praised and thanked and may He grant us a peaceful and healthy life, amen.

Offspring—1422

The following is a list of the children begotten by me.

I was single when my first son, Maso,[20] was born on 21 December 1391—this appears on the back of page 4. Before his birth I had got Bandecca with child but she had a miscarriage in her sixth month in July 1390. After that, as I have indicated on page 5, I had eight children by my second wife, Betta: five boys and three girls. Then, as I show on page 10, I had eleven children by my third wife, Ginevra: four boys and seven girls. Altogether, not counting the one that did not live to be baptized, I have had twenty children: ten boys and ten girls. Of these, Maso,

---

[20] Maso was the child born of the slave girl, Margherita, in Valencia.

Bernardo, Girolamo, Ghita and Betta are still alive. Praise be to God for all things, amen.

Caterina, my fourth wife, miscarried after four months and the child did not live long enough to receive baptism. That was in August 1421.

On 4 October 1422, at one o'clock on a Sunday night, Caterina gave birth to a daughter. We had Fra Aducci and Fra Giovanni Masi baptize her on Monday the 5th and christen her Ginevra Francesca. May God bless her.

At three o'clock on Friday, 7 January 1424, Caterina gave birth to a fine healthy boy whom we had baptized on the morning of Saturday the 8th.

The godparents were the Abbot Simone of S. Felice and Michele di Manetto. We christened the child Antonio Felice. God grant he turn out a good man.

Between eight and nine o'clock on the morning of Tuesday, 20 March 1425, Caterina had another healthy and attractive child who was baptized the following day—the 21st—which was the feast of St. Benedict. Fra Cristofano, Father Provincial of the monks of S. Maria Novella, the prior, Master Alessio, Master Girolamo, and Fra Benedetto were his sponsors. We christened him Lionardo Benedetto. God make him a good man.

At three in the morning of 26 July 1426, Caterina had a fine little girl whom we christened Anna Bandecca. The baptism was on the 27th and her sponsors were Antonina and Monna Lucia. God grant her His grace and that she be a comfort to us.

At two o'clock in the night of Monday, 28 August 1427, Caterina gave birth to a fine little girl. She was baptized on Wednesday morning the 22nd and christened Filippa Felice. The Abbot of S. Felice, Giovanni di Messer Forese Salviati, and Giuliano di Tommaso di Guccio, who had served in the same office with me, were her sponsors. God grant she be a source of consolation to us and fill her with His grace. Our Lord called her to Himself on 19 October 1430. This appears on page 30, notebook E. May God bless her.

At about eleven o'clock on Saturday, 2 June 1431, Caterina gave birth to a girl who was baptized on Monday the 4th in S. Giovanni's and christened Bartolomea Domenica. See notebook E, page 46.

Our Lord was pleased to call to Himself and to eternal life our two blessed children, Lionardo and Ginevra, on Saturday, 6 October 1431. This appears in notebook one, page 14. Lionardo had been in perfect health twenty-four hours before his death. God bless them and grant us the grace to bear their loss with fortitude.

Memoranda—1422

Some items worth bearing in mind are noted above on page 12. I shall follow them up with an account of events which happen during the course of the current year or of years to come.

We received news that our brother, Simone di Stagio, who had lived for about twenty-eight years in Spain and Valencia, had passed from this life of tribulation at the hour of nones on Saturday, 23 May, after receiving the sacraments as befits a devout Christian. May Our Lord receive his soul in eternal life.

I bought the house next to my own house on the corner from Monna Mea through a third party to whom she had mortgaged it. The whole transaction is clearly described in my ledger B on page 132. It cost me 50 florins.

I was Guild Consul for the eighth time from the beginning of May 1423. With me served Francesco della Luna, Agnolo di Ghezo, Niccolò di Giovanni Carducci, Francesco Bartolelli, and Giovanni di Deo. Agnolo died during his term in office, and his place was taken by Lorenzo di Piero di Lenzo.

I agreed to serve as Podestà of Montale and Agliana in order to avoid the plague. My term of office was from 12 April to 12 October 1424. A great number of people accompanied me there and, by God's grace, none of us got sick. I was the first to stay in the residence at Montale and

I saw to it that it was properly furnished and arranged. I acquired little wealth there but was highly esteemed by the inhabitants. Thanks be to God.

Our brother, Master Lionardo, General of the Preaching Friars, passed on from this life on Friday, 16 March 1425. He had been in very poor health. He received the sacraments and his funeral was honored by the Commune, the Parte Guelfa, the Merchant's Court, and the Guild Heads. His personal account is entered on page 116 of ledger B. I received a general acquittance from the friars and Chapter covering all transactions I had ever conducted with him. The instrument was drawn up by Ser Cristofano da Laterina on the advice of Messer Stefano Bonaccorsi on 3 March 1425 and I have it at home.

My name was drawn to serve among the Lord Priors of the city of Florence for a term of two months, starting on 1 July and finishing on the last day of August 1425. Serving with me were: Giovanni Grasso, Lapo Bucelli, Piero di Bonaccorso, Domenico di Tano, Giandonato di Cecco, Niccolò Valori, Cresci di Lorenzo, and Lorenzo di Piero di Lenzo, the Standard-bearer of Justice. The war[21] made our task extremely onerous but, by the grace of God, we left matters in a better way than we found them.

By the grace of God, I was Standard-bearer of Justice for two months from 1 March 1429. The priors serving with me were: Zanobi di Tommaso Bartoli, a feather-bed maker, Bianco d'Agnoli, a maker of wine glasses, as artisans of the quarter of S. Spirito; Riccardo di Niccolò Fagni and Berto di Lionardo Berti for S. Croce; Pierozzo di Francesco della Lana and Piero di Francesco Redditi for S. Maria Novella; Antonio di Ghezzo della Casa and Francesco di Piero Gherucci for S. Giovanni; and Ser Iacopo Salvestri, our notary. By God's grace we worked harmoniously together and accomplished a number of good things. I had a column placed in Piazza S. Felice; it was brought from the Mercato Vecchio, and the decision was taken by the priorate.

[21] Florence was then at war with Filippo Maria Visconti, ruler of Milan.

1428. Chronological notes concerning myself. The first, which appears on page 12, records how I was born on 15 April 1362. Further on, mention is made of the death of Stagio in 1374 and of how I began to work in the silk business in 1375 and of how Madalena got married in 1380. It is true that we owed Manetto more than 200 florins at that time, and that we owned nothing but the house and some old furniture. On 1 January 1385, I was made a partner in the business and was supposed to invest 300 florins in it. However, as appears on page 3, I was already in debt for even more than that, largely on account of expenses to which I had been put by Don Jacopo. I did well for several years after that as can be seen on page 2. In 1388 I got married and received a dowry and was able to pay off the debt that year, as well as furnishing the house decently and keeping almost within my capital. In 1390, my wife Bandecca died and I went to Valencia for the company. I returned in 1392. We had done well during this period, but due to the bad debt that Giovanni Stefani contracted with our company, I found myself rather short of money. In 1393 I married my second wife as is indicated on page 4. The dowry was substantial but I spent too much. In 1394 I was captured and robbed at sea and suffered considerable losses as is shown on page 4 of this diary. That year I bought a half share in the farm at Antella and neither made nor lost money. However, having left the company in 1395, I set up on my own and did well and made 300 or more florins. As appears on page 6, I bought Michele's share of Giovanni Stefani's debt from him for 600 florins with certain terms. I thought this to be a clever move, but it turned out not to be and I lost most of my investment. However I went into partnership with Michele in 1396, as is shown above on page 6. As I was short of money, I promised to put up 1,000 florins which, for as long as the company lasted, I was obliged to borrow on interest or raise in other ways, drawing money against Simone's account in Valencia by means of bills of exchange and other stratagems. And I did very well up to the year 1402, as appears on page 7. However, in 1400, I took refuge from the plague in Antella and spent more than 500 florins on the house and in planting vines. I had other expenses too, so that in 1402, when I parted company with Michele, I had about 1,000 florins. The entry indicates 1,370 [florins] but I owed the rest. That year, as is indicated earlier, I went into partnership with Piero Lana and engaged myself to invest 2,000 florins. I got married that same year for the third time and received over 600 florins cash as is shown on page 8. Thus I was able to invest that sum in the company, which meant that I still owed over 300 florins.

At this point, fortune turned against me. Simone had gone into business on his own account in Valencia and was involved in transactions with the King of Castile. I let him have great quantities of merchandise and bills of exchange for large sums of money. I had been against his engaging in this activity, but he was convinced that he was right. He let our company in for trouble, litigation and losses so that we went deeply into debt and were on the point of going bankrupt. I had to join him in Spain in 1408, and spent almost three years there and in Valencia, recovering only a tiny portion of our losses. As ill fortune would have it, the King, with whom Simone had dealt, died in 1406 and as a result of this Simone was unjustly treated and ruined. Our company lost over 10,000 florins in this affair, which swallowed up all our capital. Over and above these losses, Piero Lana was forced to pay further sums, and so was I, for I paid over 1,000 florins from Matteo's legacy. Piero brought a lawsuit against me which might have harmed me greatly and, in 1412, I reached a settlement with his heirs as appears on page 72 of Ledger B. I agreed to pay them 2,400 florins and, as also appears from the ledger, I finished paying off this debt in 1422. The interest I had to pay in this period amounted to over 600 florins. So one may say that in 1412, according to a rough estimate that I made of my losses and the interest I had to pay on account of them, I was in debt for over 3,000 florins. That same year 1412, my name was drawn to be Standard-bearer of Justice, and I served in that office. This was the beginning of my recovery. After that, in 1414, I married off Bandecca and gave her a dowry of 550 florins. That same year our brother Lionardo was made Father General of his Order. So our trust in God aided and comforted us.

After reaching the settlement with Piero Lana's heirs in 1412, I found myself in debt for about 3,000 florins. God came to my aid then with the promotion of my brother who, as Father General, was in a position to help me pay off the debt. The assistance he gave me from time to time and according to his means is recorded in ledger B, page 94. The sums he paid out to me and in my name up to the year 1420 amounted to 2,330 florins, and he made me a gift of them. There were still 700 florins to be paid off and, as my living expenses during that time amounted to more than that sum, my total debt was 1,500 florins. However, I had sold off various pieces of furniture, which brought in 200 florins; the sale of the Campi farm brought in 250 gold florins; Ginevra's communal bonds brought in interest amounting to 200 florins. When Pope John [XXIII] came, I made 150 Bologna florins from cloths I made for him, and in 1418 I made 200 florins as *Provedi-tore*[22] in Pisa. All this amounted to 1,000 florins, so that I can say that in 1412 I only owed 500 florins.

I set up in business again, and in 1421 I remarried and my wife brought me 600 florins. In the course of 1421 and 1422, the Father General lent me 1,000 florins. Michele joined my company and I did well so that when we drew up our third balance sheet on 1 January 1424, my own profit came to 1,100 florins. This profit, together with my wife's dowry and what the Father General had lent me, came to 2,700. When I had subtracted the 500 florins for my debt and further sums for expenses, I had about 900 florins left in hand. In 1424 I got money from the Father General in Cosimo's[23] name which he later turned into a

[22] The *Proveditori*, a magistracy of five citizens with general responsibility for the government of Pisa and its contado.
[23] The banker, Cosimo de' Medici.

gift, together with another sum which brought it to 500 florins, so that altogether I had 1,400 florins net. However, God called him to Himself that year and we did badly in the business. I don't know how this occurred, for I was at Montale and my losses amounted to 250 florins. Then the war started and we made very little while it lasted but had to bear heavy expenses. However, the greatest damage to me was the terrible tax burden imposed by the Commune, which cost me 1,200 florins. I had to pay back a dowry, for which I had gone surety, to Nardo di Lippo's wife. This cost me 300 florins, and I have entered this debt against the heir on page 2 of register D. I don't know whether I will be able to recover the money. So, in 1427, I was almost able to keep within my capital. I set up a new company with Michele and Giovanni di Ser Guido and, in my red account book, the capital and merchandise assessed at the cash value amounted to 1,000 florins, allowing 300 florins to pay for the furnishings and goodwill. But in my old white purchases book B, I have a debt of about 700 florins, so I have practically no liquid capital at all.[24]

[24] Dati died on 17 September 1435; he did not keep his diary for the last eight years of his life.